THE ART OF ROMANCE

Mills & Boon® and Harlequin® Cover Designs

Joanna Bowring and Margaret O'Brien

Prestel

Munich • Berlin • London • New York

This book is published on the occasion of the exhibition *And Then He Kissed Her...*, celebrating 100 years of Mills & Boon, held at Manchester Central Library 5 June – 9 August 2008, and then touring. For further venues see the website: www.millsandboon.co.uk

Authors' Acknowledgements and Note
Thanks to Joseph McAleer, Jean MacLeod, Jim Cook and Lilie Ferrari for loans of photographs and covers. The authors would also like to thank Joseph McAleer, whose book Passion's Fortune: the Story of Mills & Boon *(Oxford: OUP, 1999) was an invaluable source on the history of the company.*
The dimensions of Mills & Boon pre-1970s hardbacks are 19 x 12.5 cm; later hardbacks are 19 x 13 cm; paperbacks are 17 x 10.8 cm. The dates given in the captions refer to the copy of the book from which the cover is illustrated: this may differ from the date of first publication of the book. The artists involved in the cover designs have been identified where the information was available, and the authors would be delighted to receive any information on the artwork they have not been able to attribute.

Prestel Verlag
Königinstrasse 9, D-80539 Munich
T +49 (89) 242 908 329
F +49 (89) 242 908 335
www.prestel.de

Prestel Publishing Ltd.
4 Bloomsbury Place, London WC1A 2QA
Tel. +44 (020) 7323-5004
Fax +44 (020) 7636-8004

Prestel Publishing
900 Broadway, Suite 603
New York, N.Y. 10003
Tel. +1 (212) 995-2720
Fax +1 (212) 995-2733
www.prestel.com

Library of Congress Control Number: 2008928299

British Library Cataloguing-in-Publication Data: A catalogue record for this book is available from the British Library. The Deutsche Bibliothek holds a record of this publication in the Deutsche Nationalbibliographie; detailed bibliographical data can be found under: http://dnb.dde.de

Prestel books are available worldwide. Please contact your nearest bookseller or one of the above addresses for information concerning your local distributor.

Editorial direction: Philippa Hurd
Design and layout: Cilly Klotz
Cover design by Paul Vater at Sugarfree Design Ltd., London
Typesetting: Fotosatz Huber, Munich
Origination: Repro Ludwig, Zell am See
Printing and binding: MKT, Ljubljana
Printed in Slovenia on acid-free paper

ISBN 978-3-7913-4122-4

CONTENTS

'AND THEN HE KISSED HER ...'

100 Years of Mills & Boon® and 60 Years of Harlequin®

'Mills & Boon is a trademark that is so imbued in the British psyche. It's like Blackpool rock. It's a tremendous pull. If anyone says Mills & Boon, you know immediately what they mean.'

Mills & Boon author Jane Donnelly, quoted in Joseph McAleer, PASSION'S FORTUNE: THE STORY OF MILLS & BOON.

Fig. 1 Charles Boon

Mills & Boon, the United Kingdom's leading publisher of romantic fiction, is one hundred years old in 2008; and its parent company, Harlequin, celebrates sixty years in 2009. Over the years, both firms have become household names, their books enjoying the almost unique distinction of being requested by publisher, rather than author. In 1997, the phrase 'Mills & Boon', meaning a type of popular romantic novel, was added to the Oxford English Dictionary. The dictionary quotes a WH Smith Trade Circular from 26 July 1952: 'Without ever having read a Mills & Boon romance I know I can quite safely say to the vague customer in search of "a nice romance" – "try a Mills & Boon".'

The increase in literacy before World War I had led to a huge increase in reading, and the corresponding growth of the publishing industry was the context within which Gerald Mills and Charles Boon (fig. 1), who had been working together at the publishers Methuen, started a new company in 1908. It was a successful partnership: Mills was the chief investor with an interest in educational publishing; while Boon was more of a showman, 'the original wide boy' according to his daughter, as well as a gifted editor and marketeer. Disarmingly Charles Boon's son Alan admitted in *Passion's Fortune*: 'My father had no intellectual interest in books which was perhaps an asset – he stuck to entertainment'.

The first book Mills & Boon published in 1908 was, prophetically, a romantic novel by the author Sophie Cole titled *Arrows from the Dark*. The book received glowing reviews, despite a storyline that readers today would find less than enthralling. Alan Boon commented, again in *Passion's Fortune*: 'Her books usually featured the heroine, a pie-eyed little girl, going down to Brighton and being seduced'. Nevertheless Cole went on to write a further 64 novels for the company.

The firm began as a general publisher, releasing books about everything from travel to crafts.

In the early years Mills & Boon also published several authors who were already famous, such as E.F. Benson, P.G. Wodehouse, and American writer Jack London (see fig. 2). London, who had enjoyed famously bad relationships with previous publish-

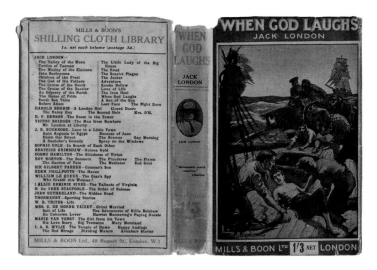

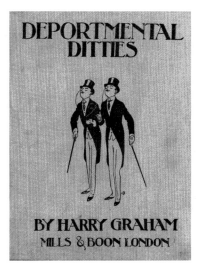

Fig. 2 Jack London, *When God Laughs*, 1912. Mills & Boon

Fig. 3 Harry Graham, *Deportmental Ditties*, 1909. Mills & Boon

ers, was happy with the move. He wrote to the company on 31 October 1914: 'You have done splendidly by me in making me popular in England. I haven't a word of complaint to make; but I do have many hearty words of thanks'.

Alongside established authors, the firm was always keen to find new writers – a policy that endures today. In 1912, for example, a thousand unsolicited manuscripts arrived at their headquarters in Rupert Street. New discoveries included Maisie Bennett, 'the Shop-Girl Novelist', who was given a year's salary to release her from her job as a librarian in a large store. And an early best-seller was Harold Begbie, who wrote under the rather progressive-sounding pseudonym of the 'Gentleman with a Duster'. In 1923, Mills & Boon published Begbie's *Life without Servants*, which aimed to prepare middle-class readers for modern life. It was dedicated to his cook (for an example of a similar book see fig. 3).

By the time World War I broke out, the company was thriving. The war also offered women increased opportunities in the paid labour market. Between 1914 and 1918, an estimated two million women replaced men in employment. The Home Front had witnessed a shift in the status of women, who were now employed in munitions factories as well as in engineering, printing and transport. Millicent Fawcett, the leading feminist, said in 1918: 'The war revolutionised the industrial position of women – it found them serfs and left them free.' This new-found freedom would be echoed in the publishing programme at Mills & Boon.

The experience of the war had stimulated reading: the London *Times*, surveying public libraries in 1917, attributed the reading boom to 'the fact that people seek distraction from the worry of the times in the reading of works of imagination'. However the prosperity of Mills & Boon was affected in the 1920s when strikes and rising book-production costs affected the entire publishing world. Mills & Boon were quick to realise that, to keep afloat, they had to find a way to increase book sales. They did this by giving readers, including growing numbers of women, what they wanted: more light fiction. The company began to concentrate on publishing hardback romances, appealing to women's desire to escape by means of a good book.

9

Many of Mills & Boon's bestselling authors during this period provided that escapism. Louise Gerard's *The Virgin's Treasure: a Romance of the Tropics* first published in 1915 (see p. 33) epitomised her typically sexy, overblown style: 'This was not England but the tropics, where blood runs hotter, and where incredible things happen with amazing swiftness'. Gerard continued to write in this vein throughout the 1920s with titles such as *The Sultan's Slave* and *The Harbour of Desire*.

Another star writer, Denise Robins, was already established when she joined Mills & Boon in 1927. Hugely popular, she and her fellow author, Elizabeth Carfrae, rescued the firm from its economic doldrums. By 1933, Mills & Boon was able to proclaim in a *Sunday Times* advertisement, 'All England is reading Denise Robins'. However, the company later came to regret its reliance on a superstar such as Robins. She left in 1935 to work for another publisher.

Reinforced by the rise of the cinema the romantic novel became truly popular during the 1930s. Cinema-going, the social habit of the age, and a very important form of entertainment, reached its peak in the 1930s and 1940s. The 1939 film of *Gone with the Wind* was an astonishing hit. Anyone who lived in London through the war remembers the constant queues which encircled the Empire cinema in Leicester Square, even on a night of bombing, when customers had to climb over fire hoses to get to the box office. It was a symbol of romance triumphing over everyday hardships.

By 1946, 73 per cent of the population were cinema-goers, half of them going once a week or more, and the majority were women. Audiences usually preferred escapism, romance and spectacle. Mills & Boon novels of this period were often told from the heroine's point of view, and there was always a happy ending, with the hero ultimately tamed by the power of love. Mairi O'Nair's *Jennifer Disappears* of 1933 (see p. 37) exemplifies this formula: 'Brian, Brian …I thought I had lost you…''And I you, darling. It's been the rottenest of times, but it's all over now. We'll get married as soon as we can and hang the consequences. I won't risk losing you again.' The book's dramatic cover places the story fully within current trends of cinema-going.

Certain popular cinema genres were reflected on Mills & Boon covers. *Take me! Break me!* (1938; see p. 50) by Sylvia Sark features a jungle scene with a hunk in a leopard skin holding a beautiful girl. In the background a lion is ready to pounce. The imagery is pure Tarzan and Jane. Other covers, such as Mary Burchell's *Wife by Arrangement* (1946; see p. 68), are reminiscent of *film noir* in its use of contrasting light and shadow, urban location and cigarette-smoking. Cinema references are also evident on the covers of Mills & Boon's output for men at this time, such as the Western *Purple Dawson Rancher* (1935; see p. 38) by William L. Hawkins.

Throughout this period at Mills & Boon the hunt for new writers continued, and they were found in all classes and age-groups. They included Irene Swatridge, who ran a sheep farm in Devon, and wrote as Jan Tempest. She was discovered in the publisher's slush pile and was promoted energetically in an advertisement that ran in the *Sunday Times* in 1935. Between 1936 and 1945, Tempest wrote seven novels a year, contributing greatly to Mills & Boon's commercial success.

Ida Cook, a Civil Service typist from Lewisham who wrote as Mary Burchell, joined Mills & Boon in 1936 (fig. 4). This was the start of a long career with the company. By the time of her death in 1986 she had published more than 110 novels. *Wife to Christopher*, her first book, was the tale of an unhappy marriage transformed into love. During the 1930s, Ida and her sister used their frequent trips to the opera in pre-war Germany as a cover for journeys in which they helped bring Jews to safety in England. Ida's new-found wealth as an author financed this dangerous enterprise.

Fig. 5 The Boon Brothers, Alan and John

Their story is told in Ida's autobiography *We Followed our Stars* (1956), re-issued as *Safe Passage* (2008). The sisters never married, and lived together all their lives.

Jean MacLeod started sending ideas to Mills & Boon at the age of 30, and ended up writing 130 novels for the company, both as Jean S. MacLeod and under the *nom-de-plume* of Catherine Airlie. The popular imagery of Scotland features on MacLeod's covers right through her career. *Cameron of Gare* (1952; see p. 93), its cover illustrated by 'Potts', has all the ingredients – tweed, tartan and heather-covered hills. Joseph McAleer quotes Jean MacLeod as saying: 'I was the only one doing a real Scottish background. I love Scotland, come from three generations of farming people and could describe it apparently.'

When war broke out in 1939 nine million women were mobilised as part of the war effort, making up a third of the workforce in heavy industry. They had to get used to going out to work as well as running the home, and this change in lifestyle affected women's fashions. Military influences, for example the wearing of trousers, were becoming more evident. Despite the need for practicality, longer hair and red lipstick became fashionable as an antidote to the war and a boost to morale, and this was reflected on covers such as *House of Glass* (1944; see p. 61) and *Will You Go with Me?* (1944; see p. 60). Despite the all-pervading war-time atmosphere, Mills & Boon novels of the period were slow to pick up on contemporary themes and stories. This was partly because at the beginning of the war no one expected that the conflict would last very long and the company feared that war-time settings would soon become outdated and this would affect sales. Nevertheless, during the war, romantic themes remained popular as readers sought escape from the troubled times. Ida Cook (author Mary Burchell) recalled years later: 'Of course we all like make believe, particularly when things aren't going particularly well'.

For some Mills & Boon novelists, however, the war enhanced the potential for romance. Soldiers, airmen and reserve workers now appeared as heroes; while heroines, called up for war work, displayed extraordinary bravery. The war in the air is shown on covers such as *W.A.A.F. into Wife* (1943; see p. 56) by Barbara Stanton, and *Westward to my Love* (1944; see p. 59) by Jan Tempest. Despite the exigencies of wartime paper-rationing lengthy patriotic statements were common in the books – another Mills & Boon contribution to the war effort.

Charles Boon died on 2 December 1943, and his sons, Alan and John, came back from the Services to run the firm (fig. 5). Tributes to their father ('how brilliantly he gauged public taste,' said one testimonial) could not, however, disguise the fact that the Boons' sales figures were in decline. By the early 1950s, magazines, paperbacks and television were serious rivals to romantic fiction. To stimulate sales, therefore, Mills & Boon began a mail-order operation. They also linked up with the competition – the thriving magazine industry – and their stories were regularly serialised in weeklies such as *Woman's Weekly, Woman* and *Woman's Own*. Serialisation affected both the style and the content of Mills & Boon novels: plots became faster and more urgent, with 'cliff-hangers' inserted at the end of each chapter. Magazine editors exerted strong control over storylines. Winifred 'Biddy' Johnson of *Woman's Weekly*, in particular, had very decided ideas. For her, heroes had to be very tall, aloof, alpha males who kept the heroine at arm's length for most of the serial. Betty Beaty's 1958 story *Amber Five* (see p. 172) perfectly illustrates the 'glamorous unapproachability' of the hero, a pilot. Writers also were encouraged to avoid stories dealing with such issues as drunkenness, deformity, divorce, illegitimate children and mixed-race marriage. Biddy Johnson also advocated 'marriage in name only' (or MINO, the acronym used by Johnson, as well as between Mills & Boon writers and editors) as a racy narrative device to permit the sexual conquest of the heroine, a conquest sanctioned by the fact that the couple are legally married, although they are in some way in conflict.

Magazine illustrations by artists such as Jack B. Faulks, Colin Orme and Philip Simmonds were purchased by Mills & Boon and used as their book covers. Alan Boon, like the magazine editors, had strong opinions on the covers, commenting in 1964: 'We go back to our nice young couple, neatly (and always fully) dressed with a bit of background, every object clearly recognisable for what it is.' Authors, on the other hand, were not generally encouraged to have an opinion on their covers, although they often complained when artists got details wrong. Alex Stuart, author of *Island for Sale* (1955; see p. 101), went so far as to suggest detailed guidelines for the cover artist, suggestions which were clearly taken up in the final artwork: the hero, Alastair, is 'six foot six, 34 years old with dark hair, strong features and a healthily tanned complexion'; the heroine, Cornelia, is 'five foot four, age twenty-five, ash-blonde hair, no accentuated curves . . . very beautifully and correctly dressed in tweed suit, moss green or lavender (NOT pink), hat, gloves, handbag, brogue shoes'.

In the style of a family firm, Mills & Boon eschewed literary agents for a more personal approach with authors. Alan Boon in particular displayed a genius for author relations, nurturing them with frequent letters, flowers, and lunches at the Ritz or the Post Office Tower. His authors adored him. He discovered new best-selling authors such as Anne Weale and Rosalind Brett, who set their stories in faraway locations, thus reflecting the growing interest in foreign travel for all classes during the 1950s and 1960s (figs. 6 and 7). Mairi O'Nair, who also wrote as Constance M. Evans, set her novel *Mystery at Butlin's* (1960; see p. 119) in a holiday camp, a popular choice for

British holiday makers. The cover, an innovative combination of artwork and photography, placed a fashionable woman, dressed in the post-war New Look, in the equally new world of glamorous holidays.

Hundreds of writers, some producing as many as twelve books a year, flourished under Alan's wing. At the time, it was one of the rare opportunities women had to earn considerable amounts of money. For many women in the 1950s, however, while most were still housewives, many were going into careers, including occupations such as nurses, air hostesses and secretaries. The foundation of the National Health Service, and television series such as *Dr Kildare* and *Emergency Ward 10* contributed to the popularity of medical romances. Responding as always to social trends, Mills & Boon heroes during this period were often doctors and the heroines were nurses, who had

Fig. 6 Rosalind Brett, *Stormy Haven*, 1961 (hardback), Mills & Boon

Fig. 7 Rosalind Brett, *Stormy Haven*, 1962 (paperback), Mills & Boon

to be depicted as above reproach, as Hilda Pressley describes in *Theatre Sister* (1960; see p. 118): 'He looked at her with admiration. Even with her blonde hair tucked well out of sight under her theatre cap she was still beautiful. Perfectly shaped brows, eyes the colour of a summer sky, straight nose and rounded chin, and a mouth that was generous and smiling'.

Hilda Pressley, also known as Hilda Nickson, was a former nurse who became a full-time Mills & Boon author, and many of her twenty-five romantic novels have a hospital background. One of her books, however, *The World of Nurse Mitchell* (1964; see p. 142), caused some concern to Alan Boon because of the suggestion of a lesbian relationship between two nurses. The book ends, however, by re-establishing 'normal' sexual behaviour, as both women find male doctors to love.

In the late 1950s, the Canadian publisher Harlequin started to publish Mills & Boon hospital romances in paperback for the North American market, starting with Anne Vinton's *The Hospital in Buwambo* (1957). Their programme soon expanded to four paperbacks per month, including more medical romances by Alex Stuart, Mary Burchell and Jean MacLeod. This trend filtered back to the UK and kick-started Mills & Boon's paperback revolution (late compared to other British publishers); and by 1966, half of their books were in paperback (fig. 8). The collaboration with Harlequin also resulted in vastly increased profits for both authors and for Mills & Boon. The author Betty Beaty said: 'I didn't realise at first how well I was selling abroad until I got a cheque for over £9,000 . . . This was a large amount at that time and I rang Mills and Boon saying I thought they'd made a mistake'.

In some cases Harlequin paperbacks featured the cover of the original Mills & Boon publication, but more often Harlequin employed their own cover artists. For their romance series Harlequin's covers tended to have tamer and more wholesome images. The cover of *Brittle Bondage* is a good example of this; the Mills & Boon paperback features a racy cinema-style couple, whereas the Harlequin version is a more literal-minded representation of the story, with a montage of the eternal triangle: a clean-cut hero, a doll-like heroine and a scheming 'other woman' (see pp. 150 and 161).

Many of the Harlequin Romance covers were illustrated by Paul Anna Soik, whose style uses hyper-realism to dramatic effect. The covers tell the story in a very direct way, often portraying the emotional highpoint of each narrative. The Harlequin

13

Fig. 8 Shop display in 1960

thrillers, cowboy and other action books use a much more daring pulp-fiction style. This is the world of tough cops, dope rings, guns and dangerous blondes. In the 1950s Norm Eastman, one of the best-known men's adventure magazine illustrators, was commissioned by Harlequin to produce paintings for their paperback covers. His style was very cinematic and he often set up photographic shoots to create the look for his artwork.

Times were becoming more liberal, and in the US blockbuster novels, such as Grace Metalious' *Peyton Place* (1956), Harold Robbins' *The Carpet-baggers* (1961) and Jacqueline Susann's *Valley of the Dolls* (1966), expressed a new sexual freedom. These novels, with their themes of scandal, sex, money and power were scorned by critics but loved by readers. Mills & Boon books also began to reflect the changing times and progressive attitudes, particularly towards sex. One of their most popular authors, Violet Winspear, shocked older readers with the underlying eroticism of her books (fig. 9). Her titles such as *Blue Jasmine* (1969; see p. 162) and

Fig. 9 Violet Winspear

Lucifer's Angel (1961) were usually set abroad and feature strong, exotic heroes – this despite the fact that Violet remained single and never travelled beyond England all her life. When asked by a journalist how she could know so much about romance, Violet replied angrily: 'I have an imagination, young man!' The 1965 cover of *Lucifer's Angel*, which shows a couple kissing, exemplified the increasing intimacy which the books now described and illustrated (see p. 146).

In 1971, Mills & Boon merged with Harlequin and the new company enjoyed unprecedented expansion and profits. The financial and marketing skills of Harlequin combined with the publishing expertise of Mills & Boon to form a stronger and more effective unit. The company began to expand across the globe and Mills & Boon novels appeared on bookshelves in the Netherlands, Germany, France, Sweden, Italy, Greece and Japan.

By 1981 Harlequin was the world's largest publisher of romance with 80 per cent of the world market, translations into 18 languages and sales of 107 million copies in 98 countries. When the Berlin Wall came down in 1990, staff from the West German office handed out 750,000 free Mills & Boons to women from East Germany.

Today a Mills & Boon book is sold in the UK every three seconds; and Harlequin sells more than four books per second globally. There are currently ten different Mills

& Boon series, ranging from *Romance* (where the reader stops at the bedroom door) to *Blaze* (where the reader starts at the bedroom door). The company has now expanded into 109 international markets, and embraced new forms such as Japanese Manga (see p. 245) and podcasts. Responsive to new markets, Mills & Boon are making available Polish language editions for the Polish community in the UK (see p. 251); and in 2008 they moved into the Indian market where they found a natural audience among a population familiar with the basic Bollywood plot: boy meets girl – boy loses girl – they all live happily ever after. As one Indian reader said: 'Romance, for a girl, is an ongoing thing until the day you die. It doesn't matter what age you are, you still want every bit of the romance that you experienced the first time you met your boyfriend, fiancé, or loved one.' So despite an increasingly sexual content, and the demands of the international market, the obligatory happy ending with the hero's total commitment remains central to each novel.

Over the years Mills & Boon readers have remained faithful to certain enduring fantasies. One of these is the sheikh as hero (see p. 243). In 1919, E.M. Hull's novel *The Sheikh* put the desert into romance and three years later, Rudolf Valentino's film *The Sheikh* continued the craze. In 1921 Louise Gerard's *A Sultan's Slave* started a series of Mills & Boon sheikh novels. Popular recent titles include *In the Sheikh's Arms* (2003), *Love Slave to the Sheikh* (2006), *The Sultan's Virgin Bride* (2006) and *The Sheikh's Ransomed Bride* (2007). The sheikhs in these books are masculine and powerful, but willing to surrender to love. The novels appeal to the longing for the exotic, the forbidden, and to a continuing, overwhelming desire which transcends race, social background, class and moral codes. This description from Gerard's *A Sultan's Slave* could appear in any of the subsequent sheikh romances: 'He appeared one afternoon riding like a madman out of the blazing distance; a picturesque figure in his flowing white burnoose sitting on his black stallion like a centaur...lean and lithe and brown, with fierce black eyes and a cruel mouth....'

The heroine, although seemingly resistant to the charms of her desert lover at first, is ultimately charmed by him, as can be seen in Violet Winspear's 1960s novel *Blue Jasmine*: 'The door swept open and he stood framed there a moment. ...He wore a rich kaftan of saffron silk swinging back from the creamy silk of his tunic. The sleeves of the kaftan were bordered with gold thread and a golden cord bound his snowy turban. His feet were encased in yellow slippers, and he looked as splendid as a prince of the Arabian nights ... Love and fear raged in her like a flame ... He was now her husband and never before had she felt so completely in his power.'

Today, the modern Mills & Boon sheikh is a rich, international businessman, but still rooted in the traditions of his desert background. And like all the other types of Mills & Boon heroes, he always ends up making a lifelong commitment to the heroine. This is the standard happy ending which readers continue to expect. The woman always wins: her beauty, courage and intelligence ensure that the man is tamed to accept love and domesticity. As Olive Standley wrote: 'Avril put her finger gently on his lips. "You'll have a home now my darling. I'll build it for you in my heart, stronger and more indestructible than any made of bricks and mortar... Our love will have lighted a fire that will never grow cold, never go out. Oh Dick, don't you see, my heart's your home!"' (*My Heart's your Home*, 1946).

The founding of Mills & Boon in the early years of the twentieth century coincided with the growing use of the designed book jacket. Increasing competition in the publishing industry had led to jackets being used as a means of selling books; and through the jacket designs the publisher could signal particular literary genres, making them easily identifiable for the customer.

By the 1930s Mills & Boon had established itself as a publisher of romantic fiction with a recognisable house style. Packaging and production were standardised for cost reasons and to promote the brand. Artist-designed brightly coloured jackets covered the plain brown binding beneath. Jackets could be daring or romantic, sometimes echoing the style of Hollywood film posters. For example *No Other Man* by Jan Tempest (1937; fig. 10) showed a 1930s dancing couple in the style of Fred Astaire and Ginger Rogers. In this period Mills & Boon books were advertised by their jackets as well as by their titles, and the cover was particularly important for commercial libraries who, unlike public libraries, kept the covers on their stock to attract their readers. Not all covers featured romantic couples: many were a literal illustration of the story inside. *Frail Amazon* by Juliet Armstrong (1941; fig. 11), for example, shows a striking double view of the heroine, first a brunette in the everyday clothes of a working woman and then transformed into her later role as a glamorous, blonde fashion model. The Mills & Boon imprint acquired a reputation, like any other commodity in a mass market, for a particular type of book demanded by a particular type of reader. The jackets depicted changing fashions over the hundred years, starting with demure Edwardian heroines and ending with today's young women – often in a state of undress. In 1923, the cover of *The Fortune Hunters* by C.N. and A.M. Williamson (see p. 25) shows a distinctly 1920s heroine, with cupid's-bow painted lips, cropped hair and a heart-shaped face. The artist of this cover was Joyce Dennys, who had started her career designing World War I propaganda posters. Her distinctive style is also evident on other early covers for Mills & Boon including *The Duchess in Pursuit* by I.A.R. Wylie (see p. 24) and *Before Adam* by Jack London (see p. 21). As the years progressed the covers depicted heroes and heroines dressed in the style of the day, from the formally dressed couples of the 1940s, through the New Look frocks and curvaceous women of the 1950s, to the uniformed female workforce – the nurses and air hostesses of the 1960s.

The covers also tell the story of enduring male and female stereotypes. The hero is dark, striking and rugged, possibly of a higher social status than the heroine and appears indifferent or ruthless, often at the mercy of a passion he is unable to acknowledge. It goes without saying that he is a great lover. From the 1930s onwards the idea of the alpha male became prevalent, as it was believed that women were attracted to the strongest of the species. Thus Mary Burchell wrote of the hero in her first novel *Wife to Christopher* (1936), that he had 'tall, careless magnificence, faintly sullen lips' and in 1985, Lynne Collins described the hero in *Surgeon in Disgrace* as having 'the broad shoulders and the strongly sculpted hands that were so skilled in healing with the knife and so expert when it came to setting a woman on fire with the slightest touch'. Cinema heroes were always a big influence on both writers and audiences; and Mills & Boon author Violet Winspear wrote with a photograph of Humphrey Bogart above her desk for inspiration. A 1960s cover, such as *Brittle Bondage* by Rosalind Brett (see p. 150), clearly demonstrates the influence of film: the hero, closely resembling Sean Connery's James Bond with his white suit and smouldering cigarette, looks straight at us. Meanwhile, a beautiful girl drapes herself around his neck.

Heroines vary from the sedate girl next door to the working woman and the glamorous beauty. But she is always young, beautiful, sensuous and witty. She is likely to have remarkable hair and her eyes are often an unusual colour (green, tawny, violet).

In the early years of the company, the heroine was most definitely a virgin; nowadays no longer. She has usually worked, latterly in an absorbing career. The cover of Ivy Ferrari's 1963 novel *Nurse at Ryeminster* (fig. 12), for example, shows the heroine centre-stage, with her red hair and startling green eyes gazing at us, dazzling and confident.

When these stereotypes meet, it creates the eternal love story so popular in the history of romance literature. That story is the basis of Harlequin Mills & Boon's continuing success.

Fig. 10 Jan Tempest, *No Other Man*, 1937. Mills & Boon.

Fig. 11 Juliet Armstrong, *Frail Amazon*, 1941. Mills & Boon.

Fig. 12 Ivy Ferrari, *Nurse at Ryeminster*, 1964. Mills & Boon.

1912

Jack London
WHEN GOD LAUGHS
Mills & Boon

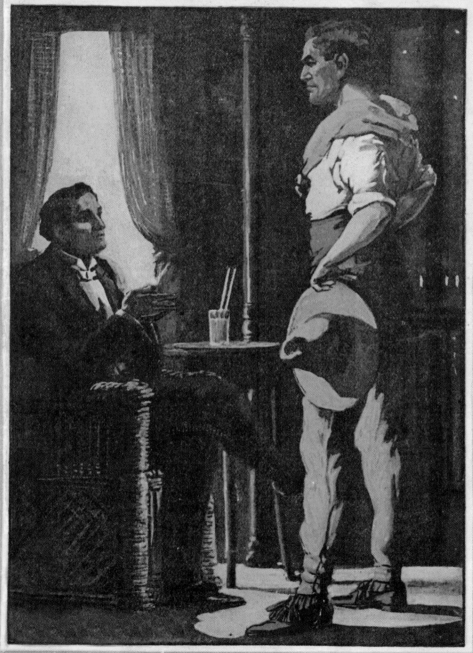

1919

Jack London
THE HOUSE OF PRIDE
Mills & Boon

THE CRUISE OF THE SNARK

BY JACK LONDON

Author of "The Valley of the Moon," "The Mutiny of the Elsinore,"
"The Jacket," etc.

JACK LONDON

"The story of THE CRUISE OF THE SNARK, as told by
Mr. Jack London with a realistic power that set so vividly
before the eyes of its readers the mystery, the charm and the
tenor of life, afloat and ashore, in the South Seas, that it may
be said to have established his reputation as a narrator and
word painter, is now issued by Mills & Boon, Ltd."—*Scotsman.*

BEFORE ADAM

BY JACK LONDON

C.L. Dennys.

JACK LONDON

MILLS & BOON Lᵀᴰ   1/6 NET   LONDON

c. 1914

Jack London
BEFORE ADAM
Mills & Boon. Cover illustration by Joyce Dennys

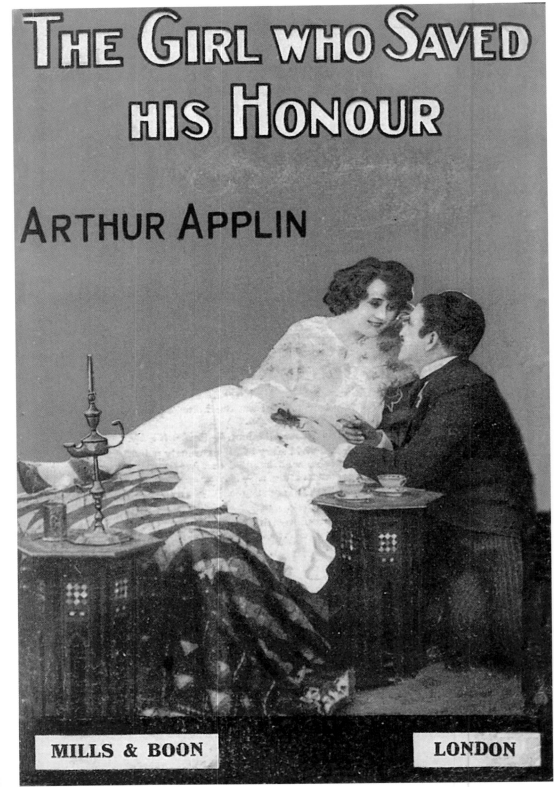

1913

Arthur Applin
THE GIRL WHO SAVED HIS HONOUR
Mills & Boon

22

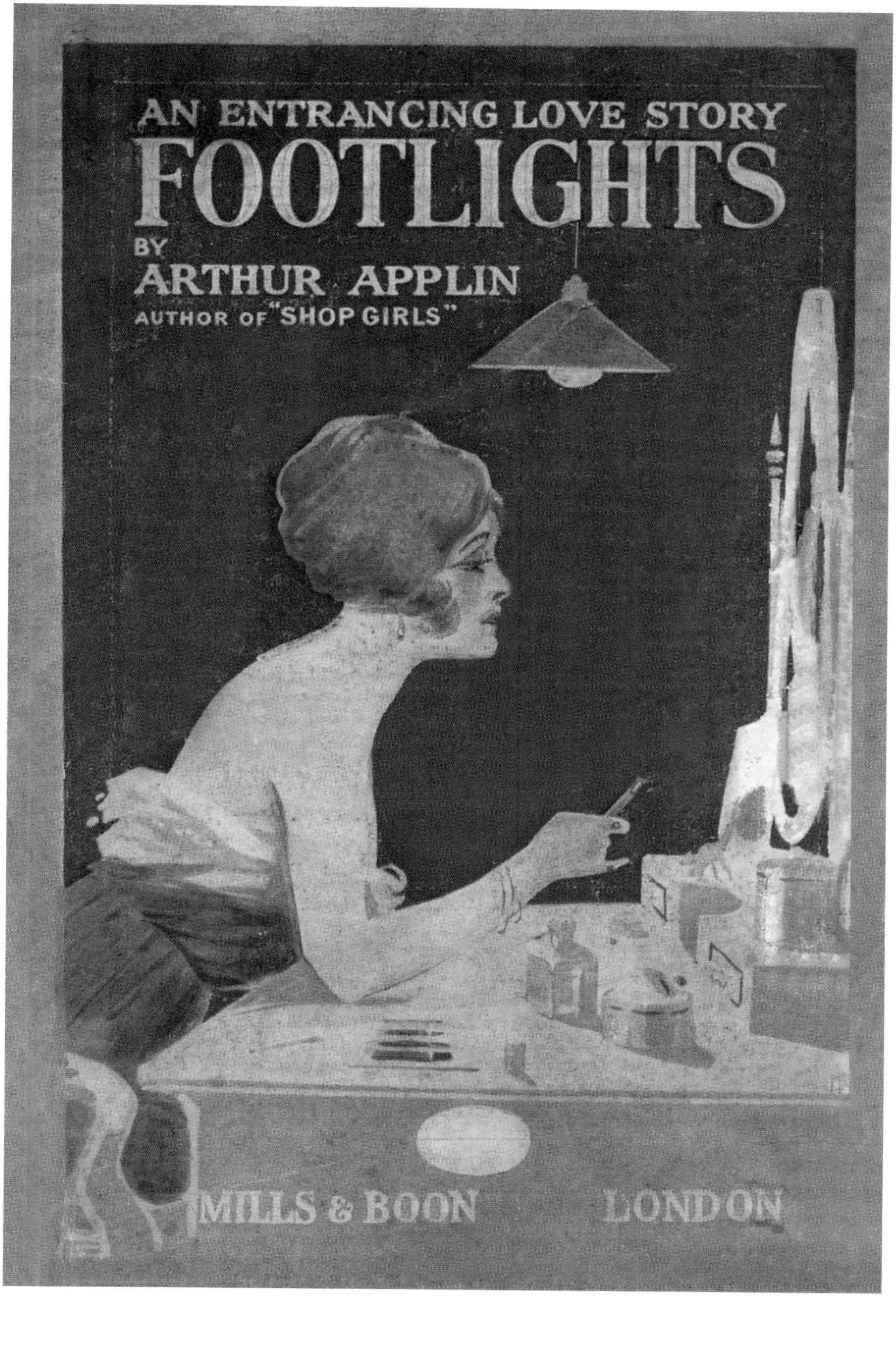
AN ENTRANCING LOVE STORY
FOOTLIGHTS
BY
ARTHUR APPLIN
AUTHOR OF "SHOP GIRLS"
MILLS & BOON
LONDON

1920

Arthur Applin
FOOTLIGHTS
Mills & Boon

THE DUCHESS IN PURSUIT

I. A. R. WYLIE

MILLS & BOON
LONDON

1917

I. A. R. Wylie
THE DUCHESS IN PURSUIT
Mills & Boon. Cover illustration by Joyce Dennys

24

THE
FORTUNE
HUNTERS

By

C.N. & A.M. WILLIAMSON

1923

C. N. and A. M. Williamson
THE FORTUNE HUNTERS
Mills & Boon. Cover illustration by Joyce Dennys

1920

I. A. R. Wylie

BRODIE AND THE DEEP SEA

Mills & Boon. Cover illustration by Harry Riley

1920

Constance Holme
CRUMP FOLK GOING HOME
Mills & Boon. Cover illustration by Rebel Stanton

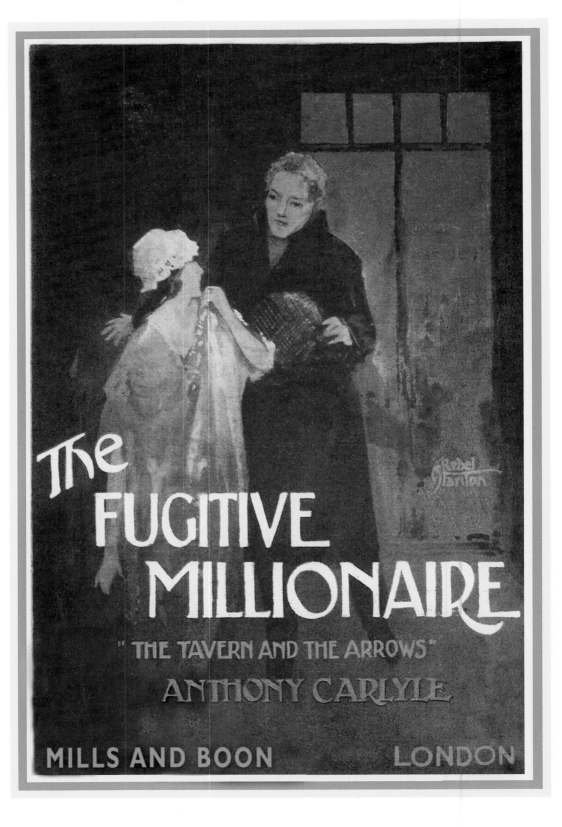

1922

Anthony Carlyle
THE FUGITIVE MILLIONAIRE
Mills & Boon. Cover illustration by Rebel Stanton

THE UNDESIGNING WIDOW

DOLF WYLLARDE

1927

Dolf Wyllarde
THE UNDESIGNING WIDOW
Mills & Boon

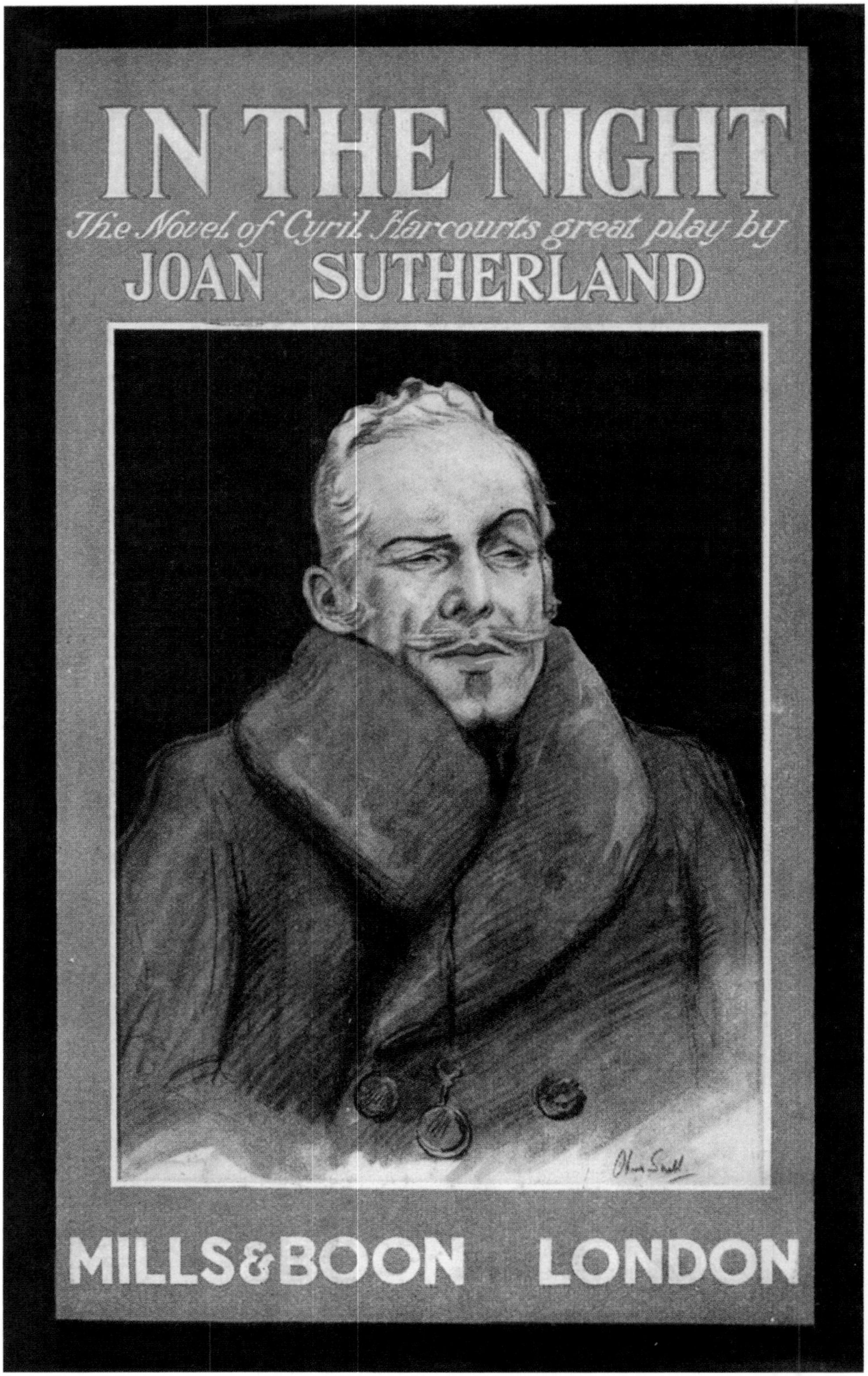

1920

Joan Sutherland
IN THE NIGHT
Mills & Boon

1926

Joan Sutherland
IN THE NIGHT
Mills & Boon

JUNGLE LOVE
A Tropical Tangle
by
LOUISE GERARD

AUTHOR OF
A Sultans Slave

MILLS & BOON   LONDON

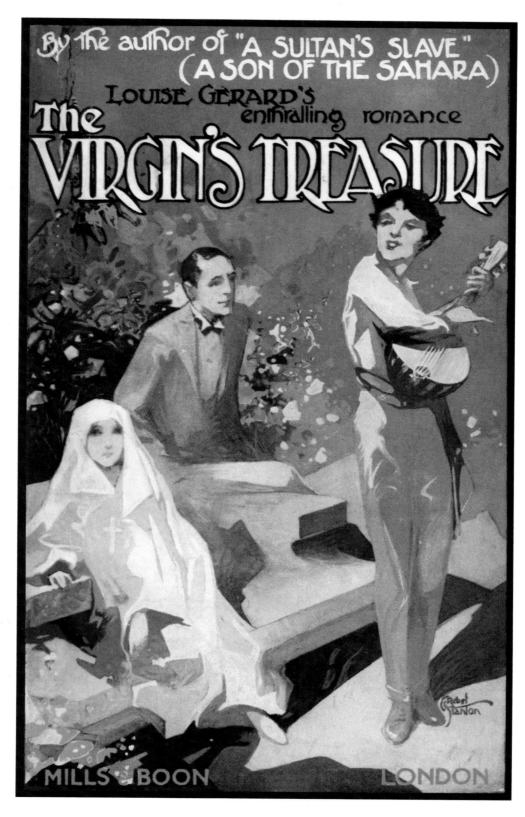

1926

Louise Gerard
THE VIRGIN'S TREASURE
Mills & Boon. Cover illustration by Rebel Stanton

1933

Sinclair Gluck
MINUS X
Mills & Boon

1934

Constance M. Evans
ROSEMARY COMES HOME
Mills & Boon

1935

Louise Gerard
FLOWER-OF-THE-MOON
Mills & Boon

1935

Mairi O'Nair
JENNIFER DISAPPEARS
Mills & Boon. Cover illustration by Sheilds

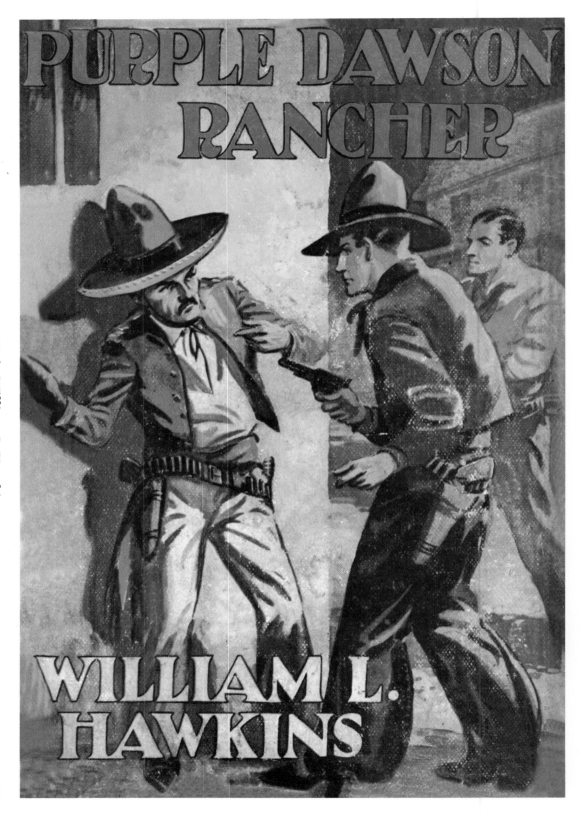

PURPLE DAWSON RANCHER

WILLIAM L. HAWKINS

1935

William L. Hawkins
PURPLE DAWSON RANCHER
Mills & Boon

MERRY GOES THE TIME

ELEANOR FARNES

1935

Eleanor Farnes
MERRY GOES THE TIME
Mills & Boon

1936

Denise Robins
DESIRE IS BLIND
Mills & Boon. Cover illustration by J. C. B. Knight

40

1936

Constance M. Evans
SECOND-HAND CINDERELLA
Mills & Boon

1936

Jan Tempest
ALL THIS I GAVE
Mills & Boon

43

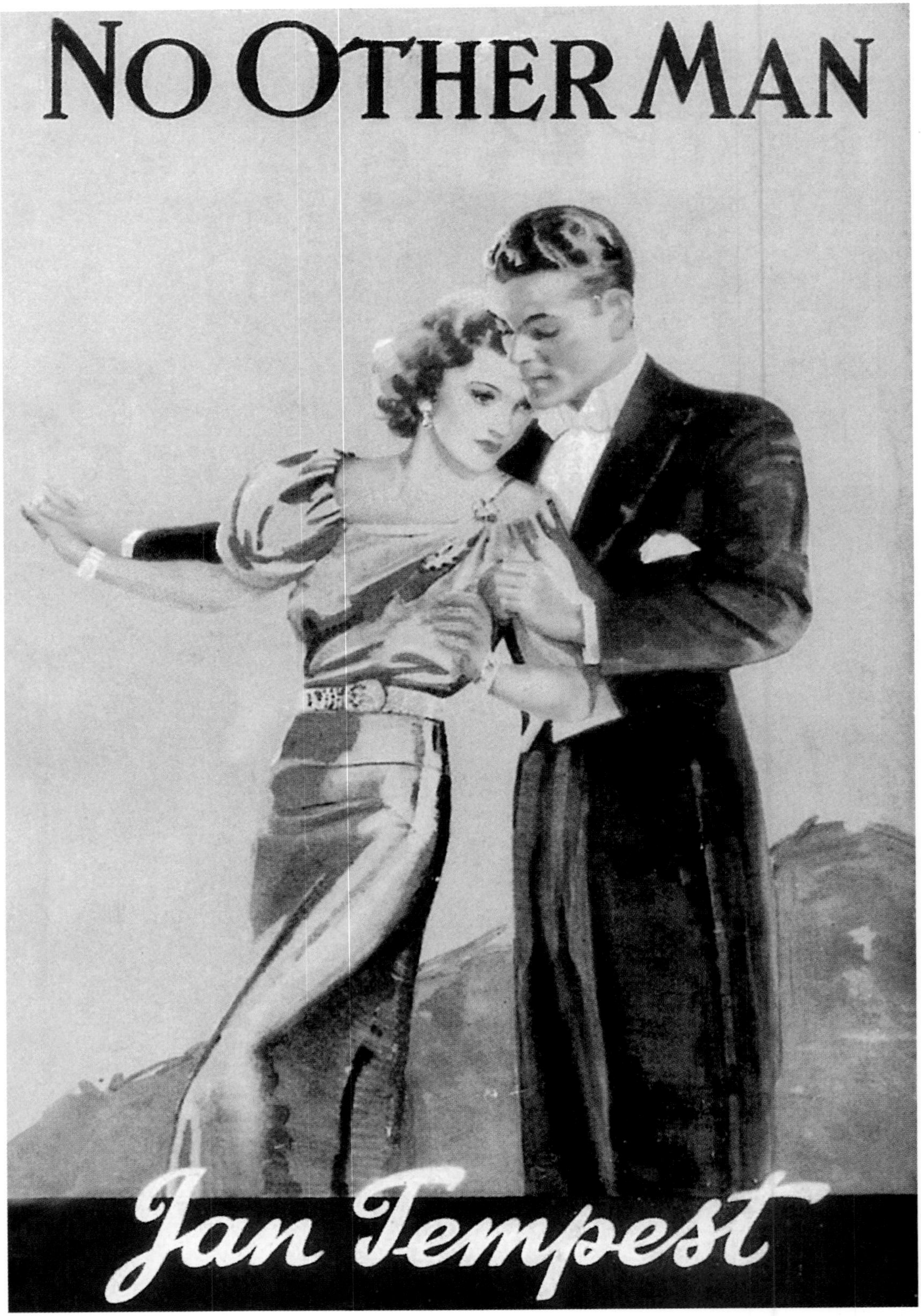

1937

Jan Tempest
NO OTHER MAN
Mills & Boon

NOBODY ASKED ME

Mary Burchell

1937

Mary Burchell
NOBODY ASKED ME
Mills & Boon

MAN–AND WAIF

Jan Tempest

1938

Jan Tempest
MAN – AND WAIF
Mills & Boon. Cover illustration by G. Fitzgerald

MIST ACROSS THE HILLS

JEAN S. MacLEOD

1938

Jean S. MacLeod
MIST ACROSS THE HILLS
Mills & Boon. Cover illustration by M. S.

WITH ALL MY WORLDLY GOODS

MARY BURCHELL

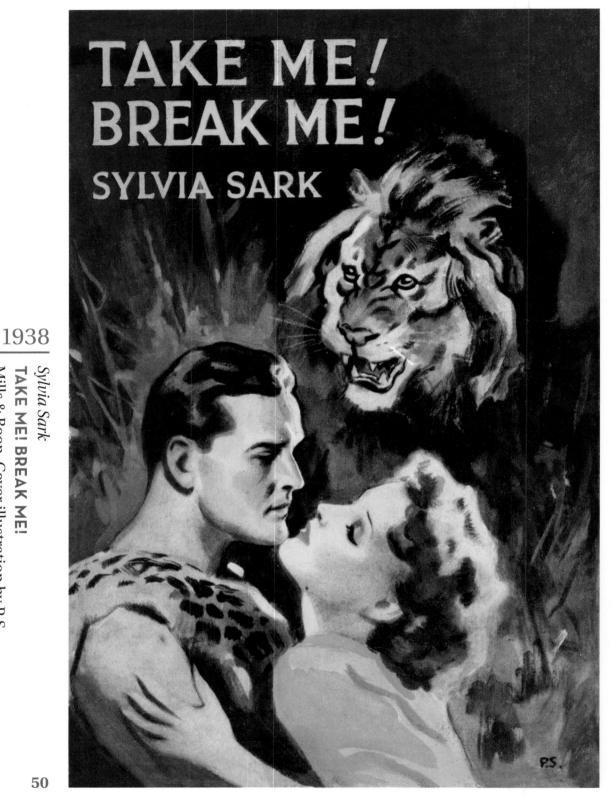

TAKE ME!
BREAK ME!
SYLVIA SARK

Sylvia Sark
TAKE ME! BREAK ME!
Mills & Boon. Cover illustration by P. S.

GRACE BEFORE MEAT

SARA SEALE

1938

Sara Seale
GRACE BEFORE MEAT
Mills & Boon

51

BLUE
SILK
SLIP

CONSTANCE M. EVANS

1939
Constance M. Evans
BLUE SILK SLIP
Mills & Boon

FRAIL AMAZON

JULIET ARMSTRONG

1941
Juliet Armstrong
FRAIL AMAZON
Mills & Boon. Cover illustration by P. S.

1942

Jan Tempest
ROMANCE ON ICE
Mills & Boon

THEY CALLED HER EVIL

FRANCES BRAYBROOKE

A MILLS & BOON LOVE STORY

1942

Frances Braybrooke
THEY CALLED HER EVIL
Mills & Boon

W.A.A.F.
into
WIFE

BARBARA
STANTON

1943
Mairi O'Nair
WHO FOLLOWS PAN?
Mills & Boon

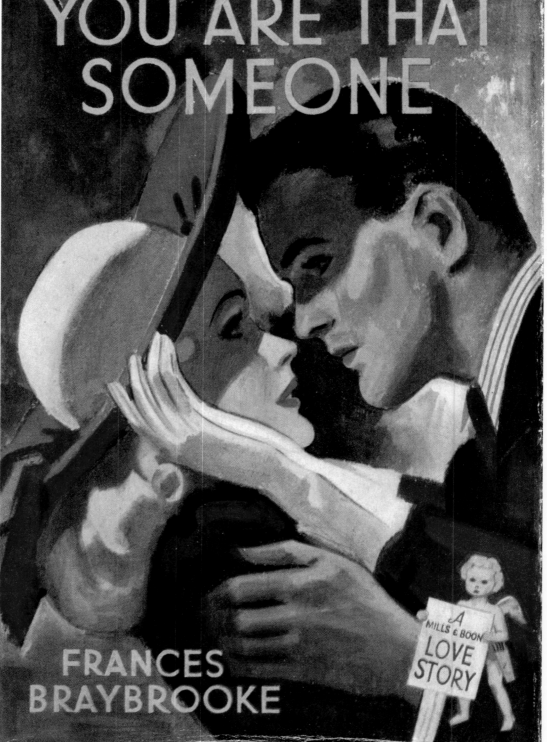

Frances Braybrooke
YOU ARE THAT SOMEONE
Mills & Boon

1944

Jan Tempest
WESTWARD TO MY LOVE
Mills & Boon

1944

Frances Braybrooke
WILL YOU GO WITH ME?
Mills & Boon

1944
Sara Seale
HOUSE OF GLASS
Mills & Boon

The
STEADFAST
FLAME

MARGARET MALCOLM

1945

Margaret Malcolm
THE STEADFAST FLAME
Mills & Boon

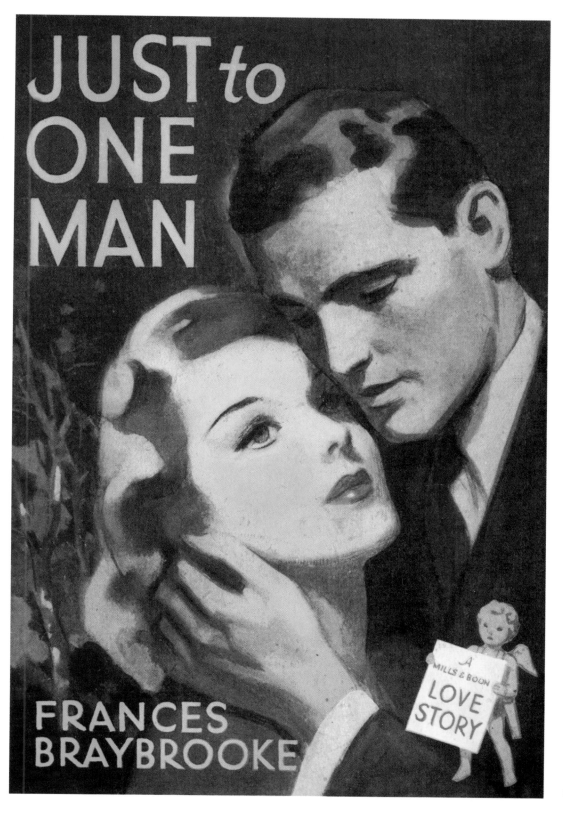

1945

Frances Braybrooke
JUST TO ONE MAN
Mills & Boon

A HEART TO PITY

MARGARET MALCOLM

1946

Olive Standley
MY HEART'S YOUR HOME
Mills & Boon

THE
THORNY
ROSE

MARGARET MALCOLM

1946

Margaret Malcolm
THE THORNY ROSE
Mills & Boon

UTILITY WEDDING
PHYLLIS MATTHEWMAN

1946

Phyllis Matthewman
UTILITY WEDDING
Mills & Boon. Cover illustration by N. L.

WIFE BY
ARRANGEMENT

MARY BURCHELL

1946

Frances Braybrooke
YOU SHALL BE MINE
Mills & Boon

1947

Margaret Malcolm
FOLLY HALL
Mills & Boon. Cover illustration by N. L.

70

1947

Margaret Malcolm
LOVE IS A GIFT
Mills & Boon. Cover illustration by N. L.

PRIDE
BEFORE
FALL

NAN SHARPE

1947

Nan Sharpe
PRIDE BEFORE FALL
Mills & Boon

The HOUSE
of
OLIVER

JEAN S. MACLEOD

1947

Jean S. Macleod
THE HOUSE OF OLIVER
Mills & Boon

TINSEL STAR

NINA BRADSHAW

1947

Nina Bradshaw
TINSEL STAR
Mills & Boon

74

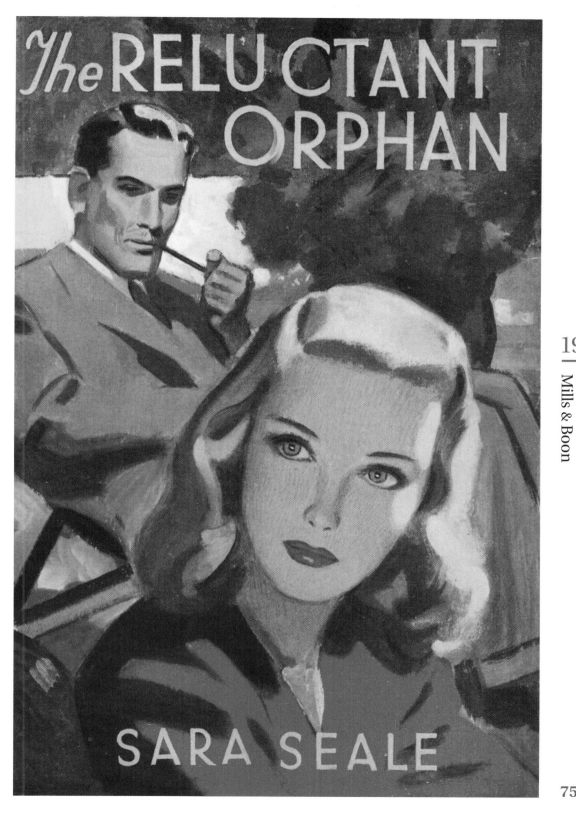

The RELUCTANT ORPHAN

SARA SEALE

1947

Sara Seale
THE RELUCTANT ORPHAN
Mills & Boon

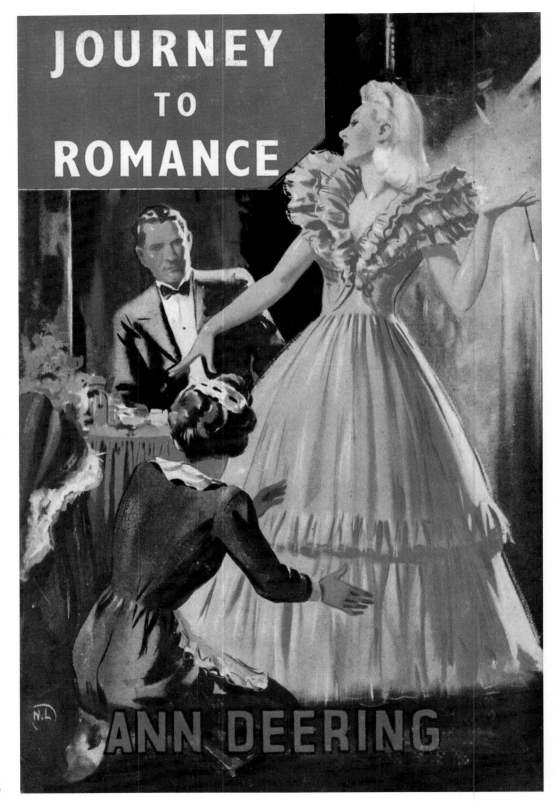

1947

Ann Deering
JOURNEY TO ROMANCE
Mills & Boon. Cover illustration by N. L.

1947

Mairi O'Nair
NIGHT CLUB HOSTESS

The
ENGLISH
TUTOR

SARA SEALE

MELODY IN TUNE

MARGARET MALCOLM

1948

Margaret Malcolm
MELODY IN TUNE
Mills & Boon

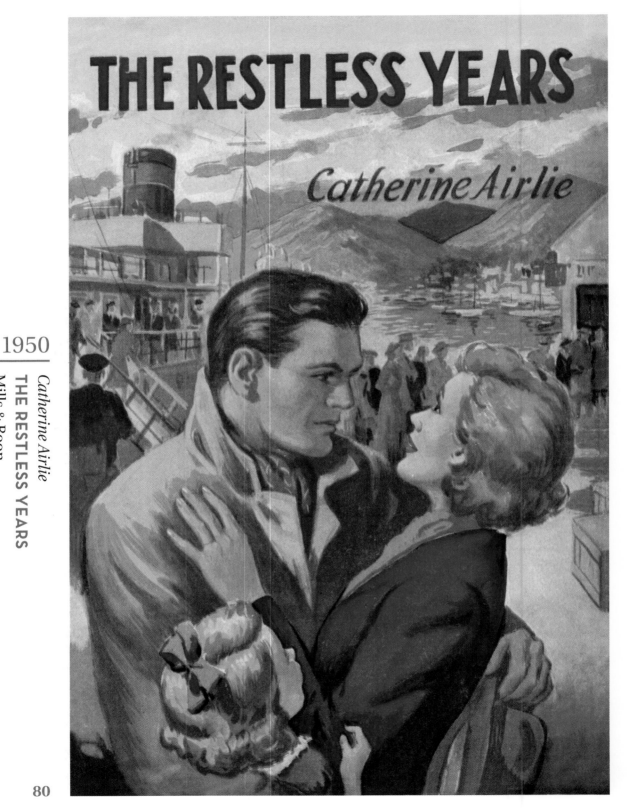

1950

Catherine Airlie
THE RESTLESS YEARS
Mills & Boon

1950

Don Macmillan
RINK RAT
Harlequin

1950

Alan Handley
KISS YOUR ELBOW
Harlequin

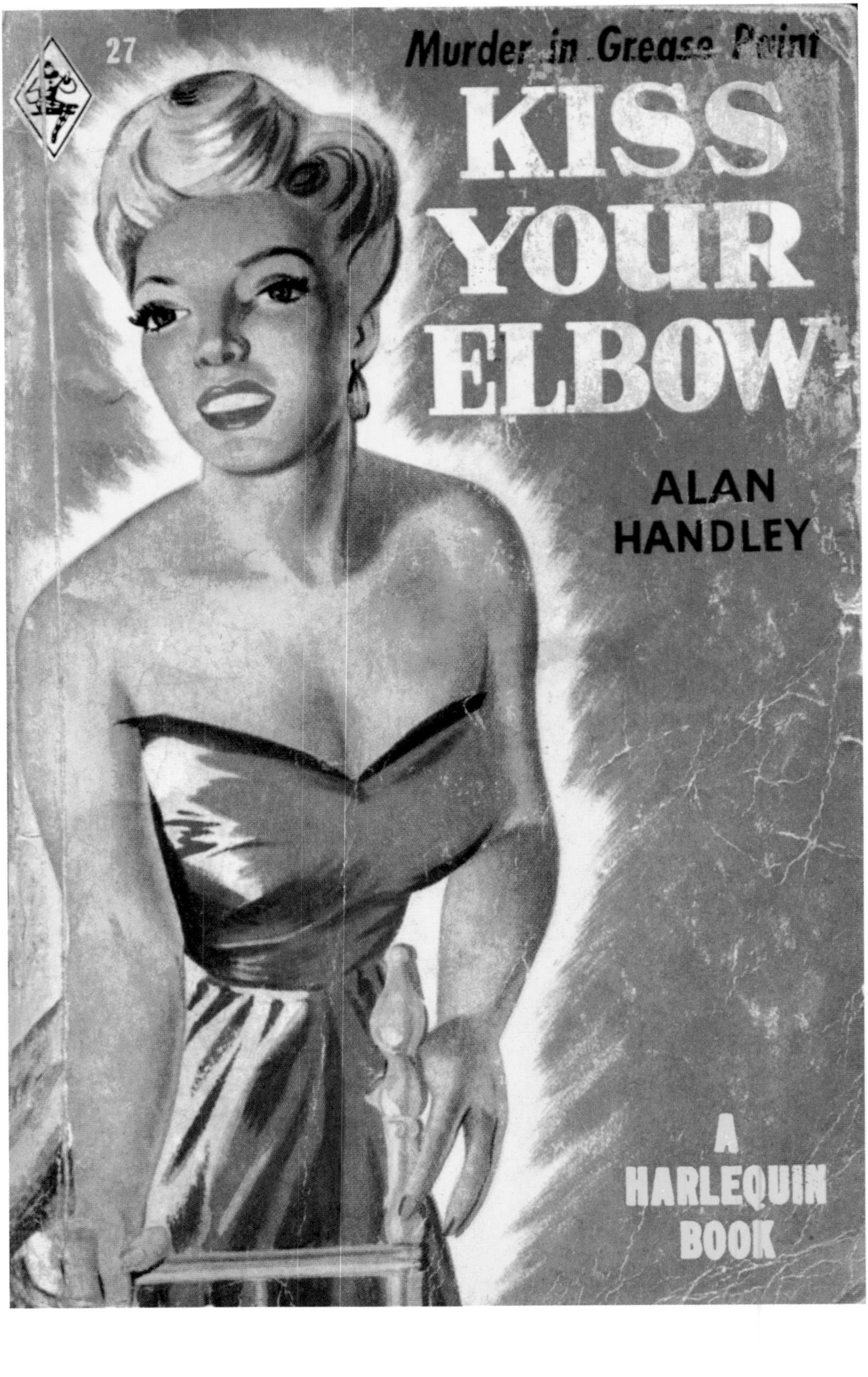
27
Murder in Grease Paint
KISS
YOUR
ELBOW
ALAN
HANDLEY
A
HARLEQUIN
BOOK

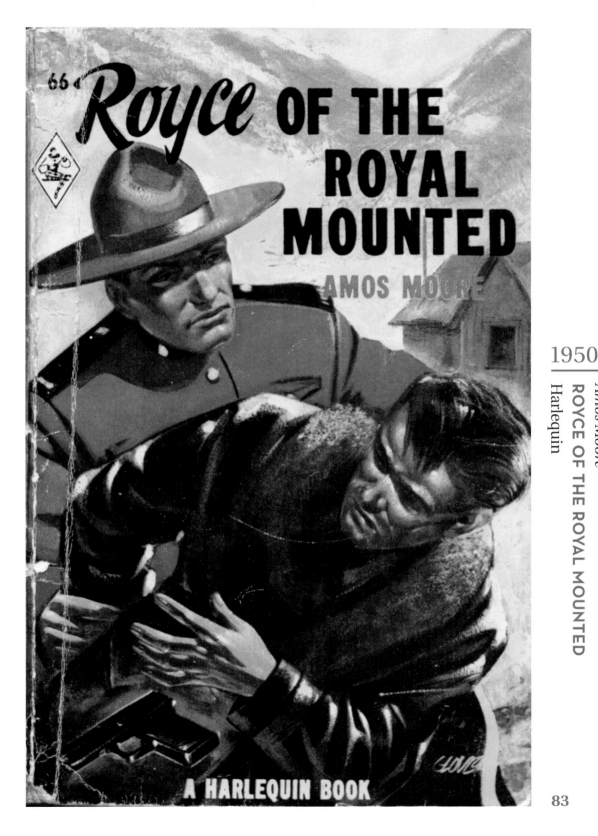

Royce OF THE ROYAL MOUNTED

AMOS MOORE

A HARLEQUIN BOOK

1950

Amos Moore
ROYCE OF THE ROYAL MOUNTED
Harlequin

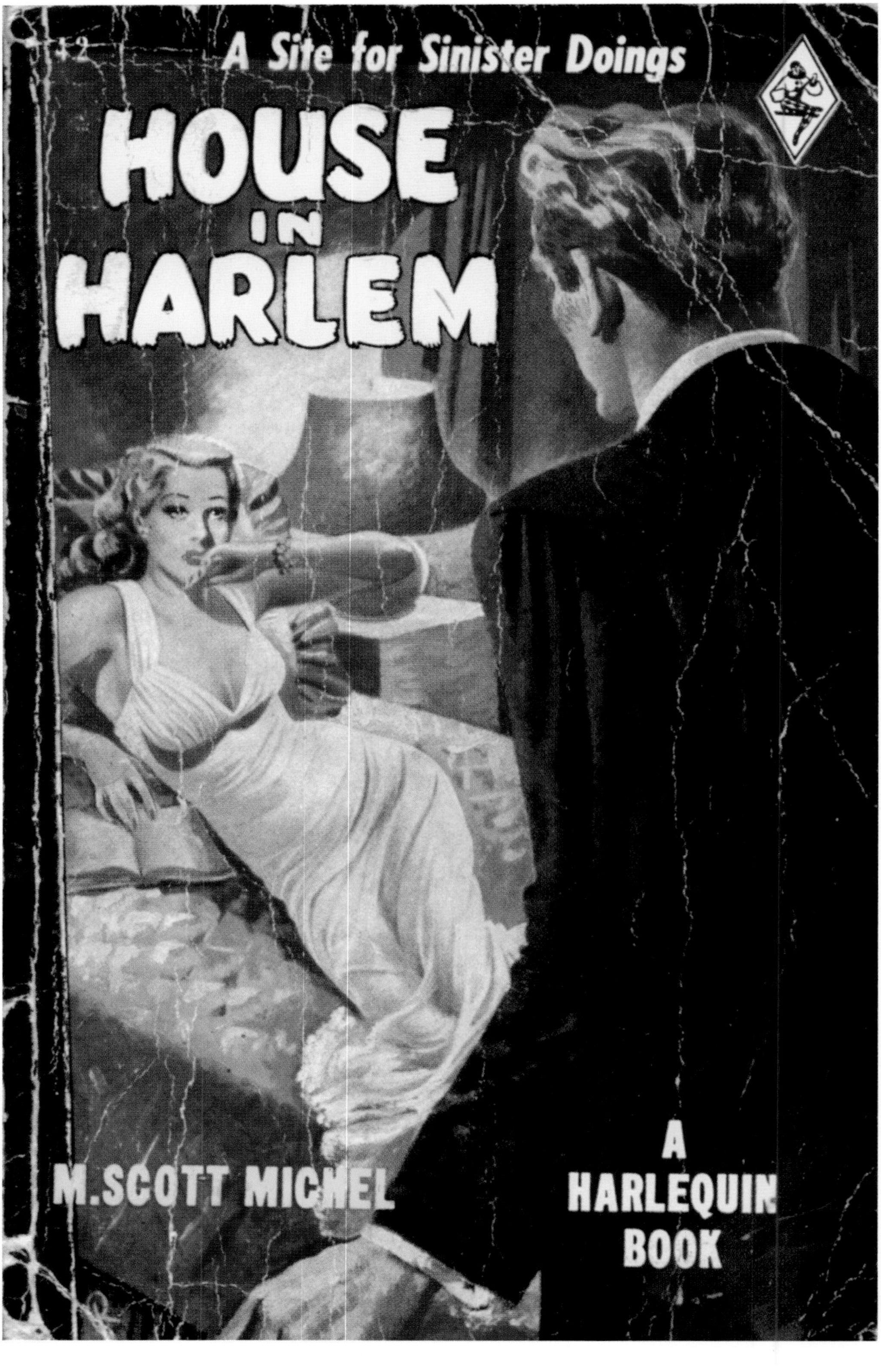
A Site for Sinister Doings
HOUSE IN HARLEM
M.SCOTT MICHEL
A HARLEQUIN BOOK

1950

M. Scott Michel
HOUSE IN HARLEM
Harlequin

69

Payoff IN BLACK

A HARLEQUIN BOOK

WILLIAM G. SCHOFIELD

1950

William G. Schofield
PAYOFF IN BLACK
Harlequin

Love for a Ship - - And for a Lady

MOBTOWN CLIPPER

S.S. RABL

A HARLEQUIN BOOK

1950

Barbara Stanton
CAN LOVE COME TWICE?
Mills & Boon

1951

Jean S. MacLeod
ROADWAY TO THE PAST
Mills & Boon

95

You're lonely when you're dead

JAMES HADLEY CHASE

A HARLEQUIN BOOK

1951

James Hadley Chase
YOU'RE LONELY WHEN YOU'RE DEAD
Harlequin

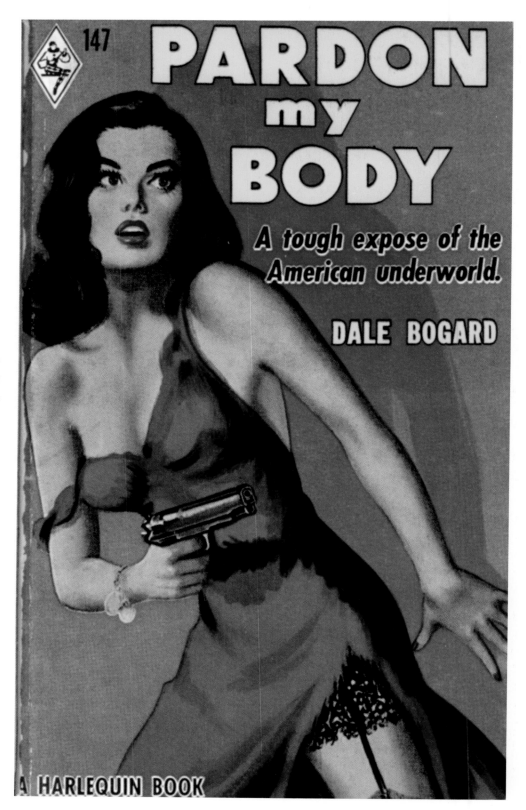

147

PARDON my BODY

A tough expose of the American underworld.

DALE BOGARD

A HARLEQUIN BOOK

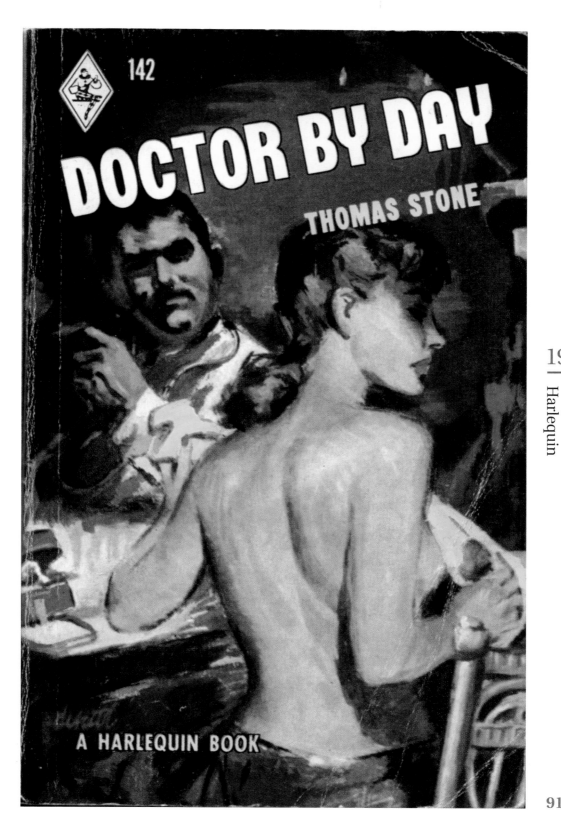

142

DOCTOR BY DAY

THOMAS STONE

A HARLEQUIN BOOK

1951

Thomas Stone
DOCTOR BY DAY
Harlequin

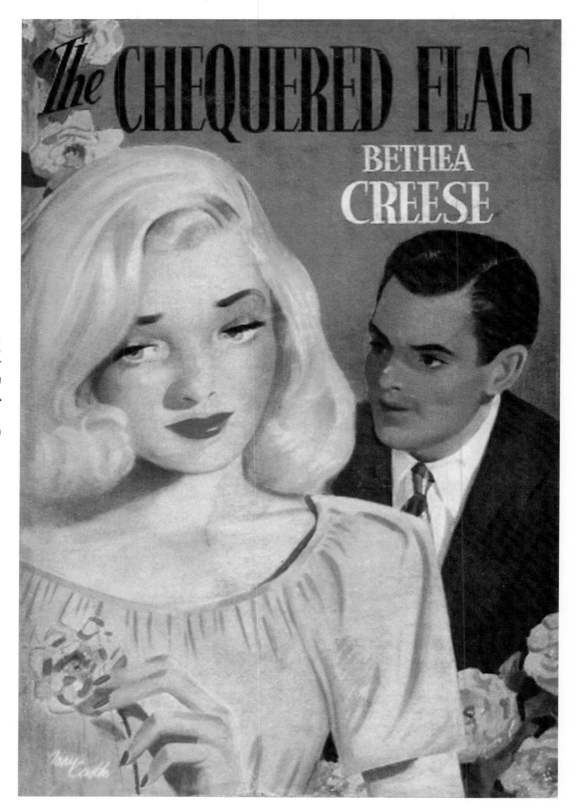

1952

Jean S. MacLeod
CAMERON OF GARE
Mills & Boon

1953

James Hadley Chase
YOU NEVER KNOW WITH WOMEN
Harlequin

233 EXPOSÉ.... Dope Rings in Canada

DIE WITH ME LADY

35¢

Ronald Cocking

A HARLEQUIN BOOK

1953

Ronald Cocking
DIE WITH ME LADY
Harlequin

235

GENERAL DUTY NURSE

LUCY AGNES
HANCOCK

WAR
C

35¢

A HARLEQUIN BOOK

1953

Lucy Agnes Hancock
GENERAL DUTY NURSE
Harlequin

1953

Jean S. MacLeod
THE SILENT VALLEY
Mills & Boon

1954

Jean S. MacLeod

THE MAN IN AUTHORITY

Mills & Boon

THE MAN IN
AUTHORITY

JEAN S. MACLEOD

DOCTORS ARE DIFFERENT

FAY CHANDOS

1954

Fay Chandos
DOCTORS ARE DIFFERENT
Mills & Boon

336

THE GOOD AND THE BAD

Joan Fleming

A HARLEQUIN BOOK

COMPLETE AND UNABRIDGED

1955

Joan Fleming
THE GOOD AND THE BAD
Harlequin

1955

Alex Stuart
ISLAND FOR SALE
Mills & Boon

BEGIN TO LIVE

ELEANOR BURFORD

1956

Eleanor Burford
BEGIN TO LIVE
Mills & Boon

ROMANCE
GOES
TENTING

PHYLLIS MATTHEWMAN

1956
Phyllis Matthewman
ROMANCE GOES TENTING
Mills & Boon

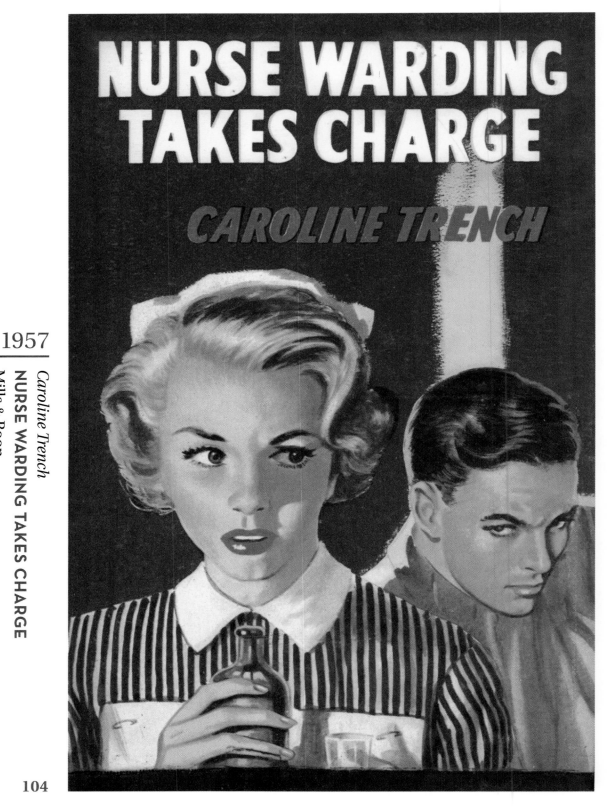

NURSE WARDING TAKES CHARGE

CAROLINE TRENCH

SWEET BARBARY

1957

Pamela Kent
SWEET BARBARY
Mills & Boon

388

by the author of *"Nurse Ellen"*

35c

DOCTOR SCOTT

PEGGY DERN

COMPLETE AND
UNABRIDGED

A HARLEQUIN BOOK

ON CALL, SISTER!

ELIZABETH GILZEAN

1958
Elizabeth Gilzean
ON CALL, SISTER!
Mills & Boon

107

1958
Catherine Airlie
RED LOTUS
Mills & Boon

644

MILLS & BOON

3'6

Never to Love

Anne Weale

1958

Anne Weale

NEVER TO LOVE

Mills & Boon

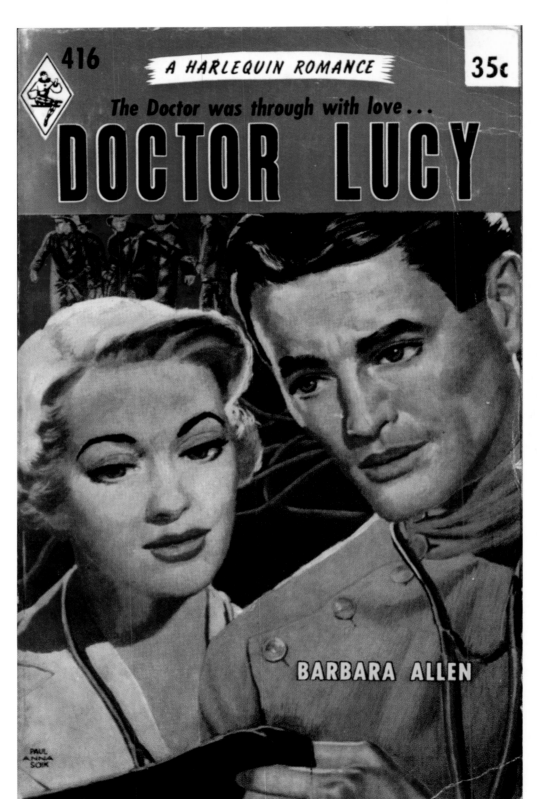

416

A HARLEQUIN ROMANCE

35c

The Doctor was through with love...

DOCTOR LUCY

BARBARA ALLEN

PAUL ANNA SOK

RED SKY AT NIGHT

ELEANOR BURFORD

1959
Eleanor Burford
RED SKY AT NIGHT
Mills & Boon

Mills & Boon

LOVE IN THE AFTERNOON

Rose Burghley

1959

SILVERTIDE
Maureen Heeley
Mills & Boon

1959
Constance M. Evans
WARD TO ANDREW
Mills & Boon

CATHERINE
AIRLIE

THE LAST OF
THE KINTYRES

1959

Catherine Airlie
THE LAST OF THE KINTYRES
Mills & Boon

THE PRISONER OF LOVE

JEAN S. MACLEOD

1960

Jean S. Macleod
THE PRISONER OF LOVE
Mills & Boon

THEATRE SISTER
Hilda Pressley

MYSTERY
at BUTLIN'S
MAIRI O'NAIR

1960
Mairi O'Nair
MYSTERY AT BUTLINS
Mills & Boon

THE LITTLE DOCTOR

JEAN S. MACLEOD

JACK M. FAULKS

1960

Jean S. MacLeod
THE LITTLE DOCTOR
Mills & Boon. Cover illustration by Jack M. Faulks

120

538

A HARLEQUIN ROMANCE

35c

Strange Request

Marjorie Bassett

1960

Marjorie Bassett
STRANGE REQUEST
Mills & Boon

THE WHITE COCKADE

JEAN S. MACLEOD

1960

Jean S. MacLeod
THE WHITE COCKADE
Mills & Boon

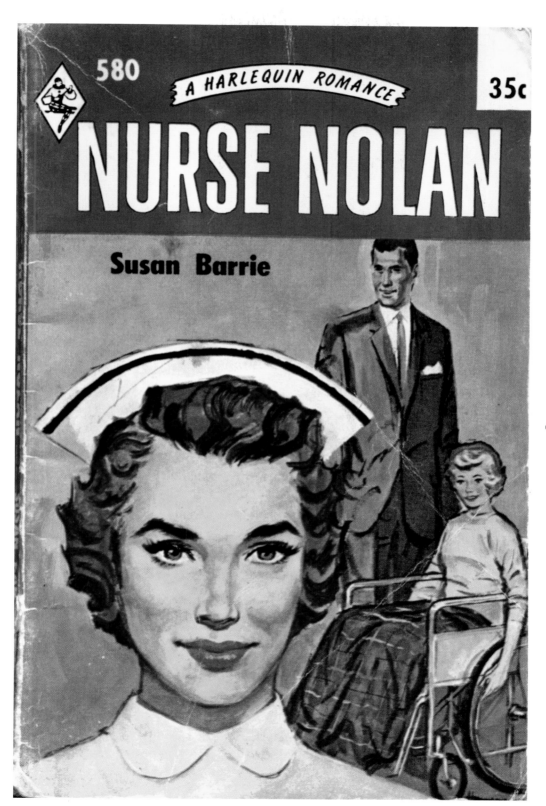

580

A HARLEQUIN ROMANCE

35c

NURSE NOLAN

Susan Barrie

1961

Susan Barrie
NURSE NOLAN
Harlequin

1961
Pamela Kent
FLIGHT TO THE STARS
Harlequin

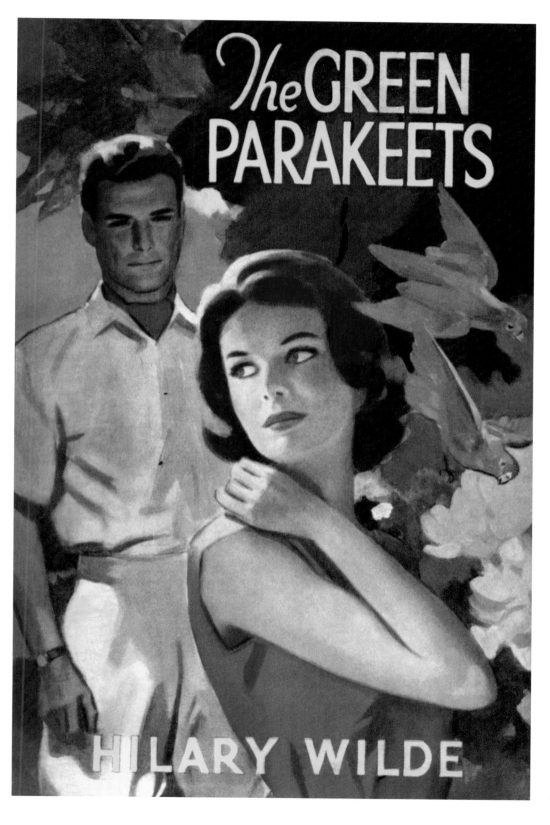

The GREEN PARAKEETS

HILARY WILDE

1961

Hilary Wilde
THE GREEN PARAKEETS
Mills & Boon

CUPID UNDER
CAPRICORN

PHYLLIS MATTHEWMAN

1961

Phyllis Mattheuman
CUPID UNDER CAPRICORN
Mills & Boon

Mills & Boon

THE HOUSE ON FLAMINGO CAY

Anne Weale

2'6 net

1962

Vivian Stuart
DOCTOR IN THE TROPICS
Harlequin

HEART, HAVE YOU NO WISDOM?

ELIZABETH HOY

1962

Elizabeth Hoy
HEART, HAVE YOU NO WISDOM?
Mills & Boon

130

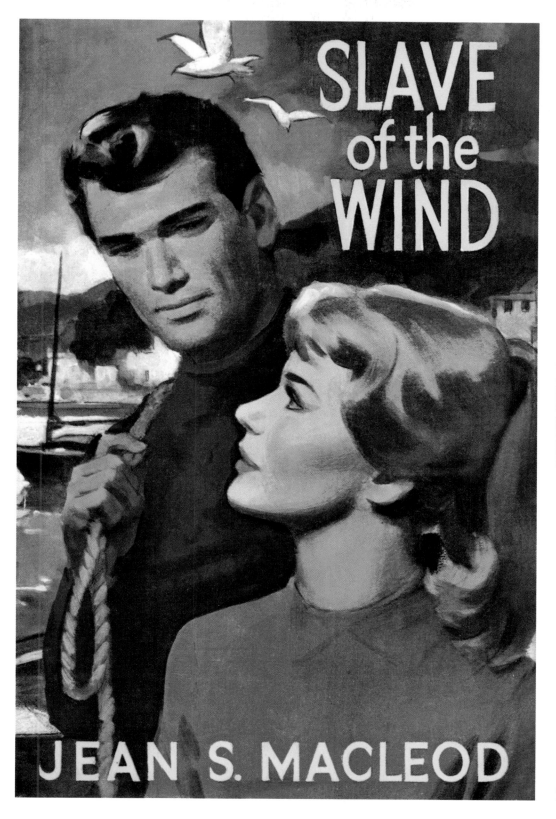

SLAVE of the WIND

JEAN S. MACLEOD

1962

Jean S. MacLeod
SLAVE OF THE WIND
Mills & Boon

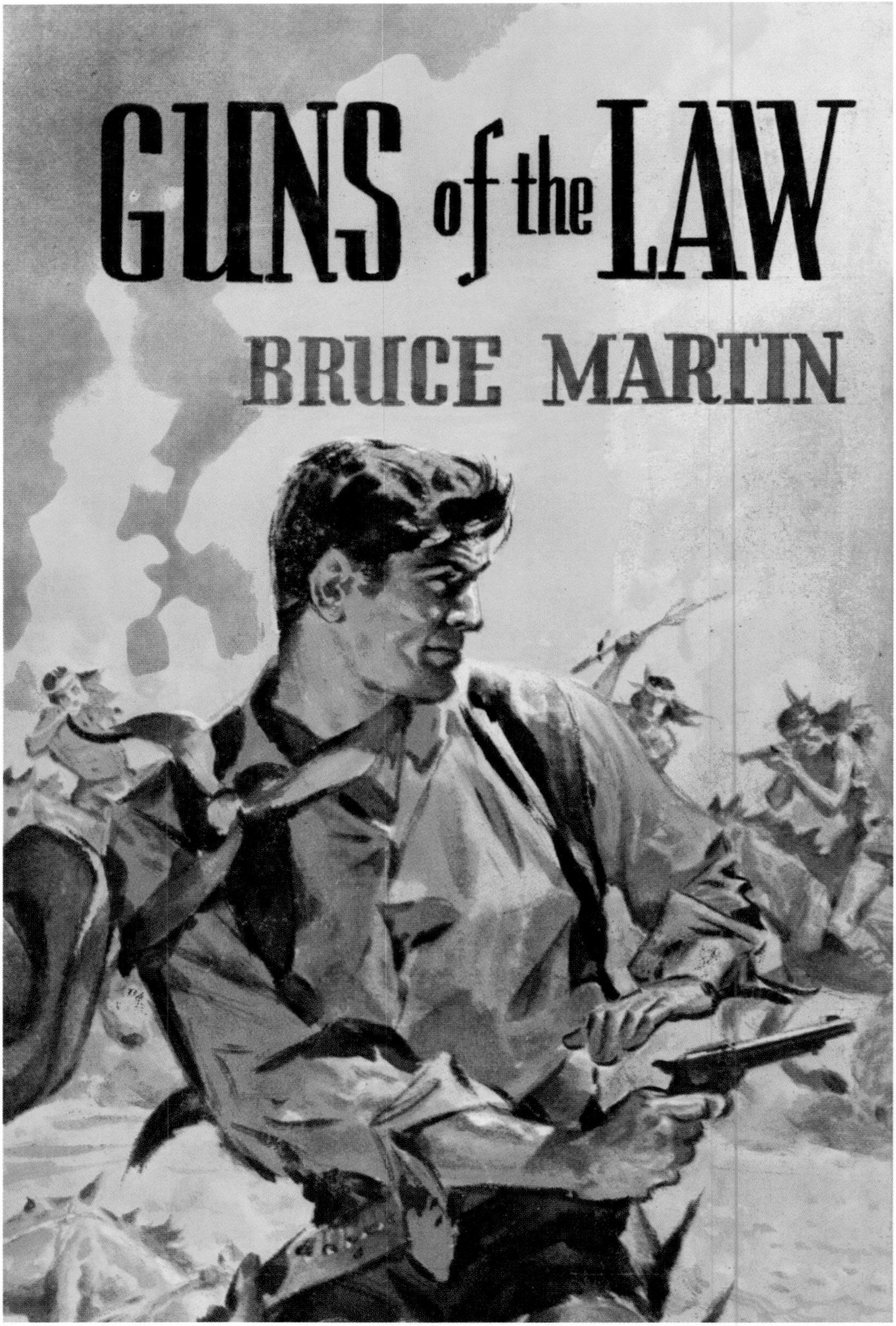
GUNS of the LAW
BRUCE MARTIN

777

A HARLEQUIN ROMANCE

40c

Scatterbrains-
STUDENT NURSE

Margaret Malcolm

1963

Margaret Malcolm
SCATTERBRAINS – STUDENT NURSE
Harlequin

DATING

WITHOUT TEARS

by
JOAN BIGGAR

1963

Joan Biggar
DATING WITHOUT TEARS
Mills & Boon

Mills & Boon

HOUSE SURGEON AT ST. ANNE'S

Mary Hunton

2/6
net

JACK M.
FAULKS

1963

Mary Hunton
HOUSE SURGEON AT ST. ANNE'S
Mills & Boon. Cover illustration by Jack M. Faulks

Mills & Boon

NURSE AT RYEMINSTER

Ivy Ferrari

JACK M.
FAULKS.

2/6
net

1964

Ivy Ferrari
NURSE AT RYEMINSTER
Mills & Boon. Cover illustration by Jack M. Faulks

136

1964

Constance M. Evans
THE FIVE-SHILLING HOLIDAY
Mills & Boon

Mills & Boon

THE TIMBER MAN

Joyce Dingwell

SUGAR ISLAND

JEAN S. MACLEOD

1964

Jean S. MacLeod
SUGAR ISLAND
Mills & Boon

DOCTOR AT RYEMINSTER

IVY FERRARI

1964

Ivy Ferrari
DOCTOR AT RYEMINSTER
Mills & Boon. Cover illustration by Jack M. Faulks

THE PATH OF THE MOONFISH

BETTY BEATY

1964

Betty Beaty
THE PATH OF THE MOONFISH
Mills & Boon

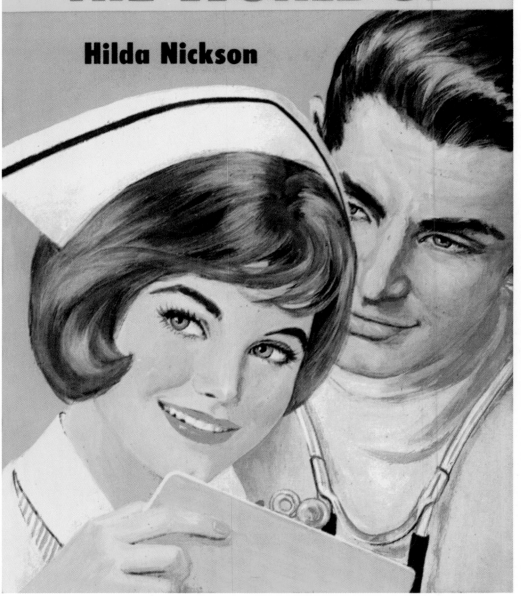

820

A HARLEQUIN ROMANCE

40c

THE WORLD OF
NURSE MITCHELL

Hilda Nickson

1964

Essie Summers
THE SMOKE AND THE FIRE
Mills & Boon

THE TENDER GLORY

JEAN S. MACLEOD

902

A HARLEQUIN ROMANCE

40c

MOUNTAIN OF DREAMS

Barbara Rowan

1965

Barbara Rowan
MOUNTAIN OF DREAMS
Harlequin

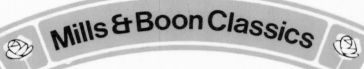

Mills & Boon Classics

Violet Winspear

LUCIFER'S ANGEL

Mills & Boon 857

LUCIFER'S ANGEL

Violet Winspear

972   A HARLEQUIN ROMANCE   45¢

BARBARY MOON

Kathryn Blair

THE STEPSISTERS

ELEANOR FARNES

1966

Eleanor Farnes
THE STEPSISTERS
Mills & Boon

Mills & Boon

BRITTLE BONDAGE

Rosalind Brett

3/6 net

Mills & Boon

THE GARDEN OF PERSEPHONE

Nan Asquith

1043

MILLS & BOON

3'6

MARRY A STRANGER

Susan Barrie

1135

A HARLEQUIN ROMANCE

.75

THERE WILL COME A STRANGER

Dorothy Rivers

1967

Dorothy Rivers
THERE WILL COME A STRANGER
Harlequin

Jill Tahourdin
WELCOME TO PARADISE
Mills & Boon

799

MILLS & BOON

3'6

LOVE IS FOR EVER

Barbara Rowan

1967

Barbara Rowan
LOVE IS FOR EVER
Mills & Boon

Mills & Boon

WHERE NO STARS SHINE

Ivy Ferrarl

1244
A HARLEQUIN ROMANCE
50¢

WHEN LOVE IS BLIND

Mary Burchell

1968

Mary Burchell
WHEN LOVE IS BLIND
Harlequin

51206

A HARLEQUIN ROMANCE

50c

SUBSTITUTE FOR LOVE

Henrietta Reid

KEEPER OF THE HEART

GWEN WESTWOOD

1969

Gwen Westwood
KEEPER OF THE HEART
Mills & Boon

PEPPERCORN HARVEST

IVY FERRARI

1969

Ivy Ferrari
PEPPERCORN HARVEST
Mills & Boon

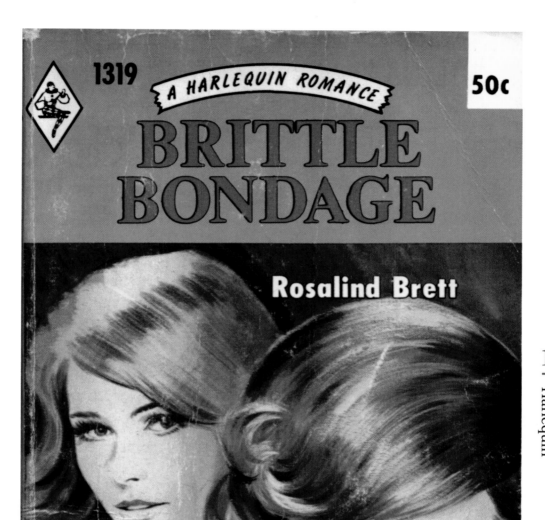

1319

A HARLEQUIN ROMANCE

50c

BRITTLE BONDAGE

Rosalind Brett

Mills & Boon

BLUE JASMINE

Violet Winspear

Mills & Boon

PARISIAN ADVENTURE

Elizabeth Ashton

MY HEART'S A DANCER

ROBERTA LEIGH

5-1548

A HARLEQUIN ROMANCE

50¢

HALFWAY TO THE STARS

Jane Donnelly

bern smith

1971

Jane Donnelly
HALFWAY TO THE STARS
Harlequin

Mills & Boon

INTO A GOLDEN LAND

Elizabeth Hoy

Mills & Boon

723

BRIDE OF THE RIF

Margaret Rome

1972

Margaret Rome
BRIDE OF THE RIF
Mills & Boon

167

Mills & Boon

THE PAGAN ISLAND

Violet Winspear

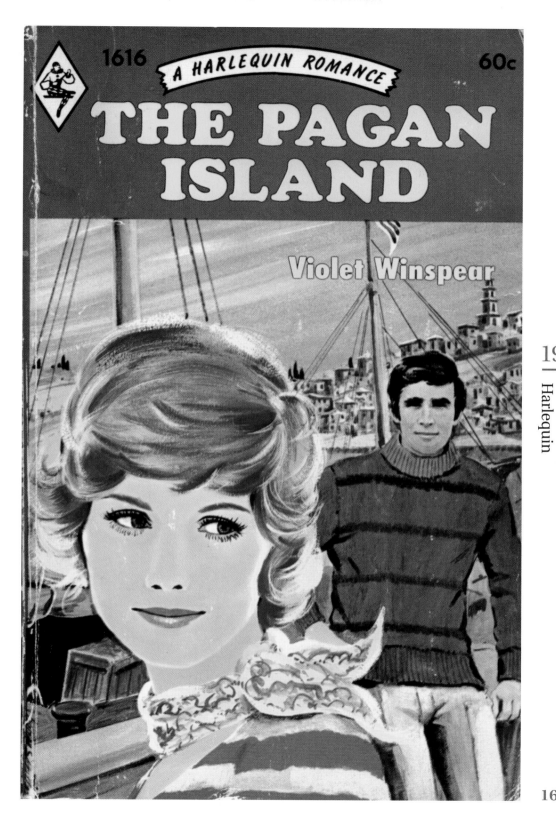

1616

A HARLEQUIN ROMANCE

60c

THE PAGAN ISLAND

Violet Winspear

1972

Violet Winspear
THE PAGAN ISLAND
Harlequin

MAIDEN FLIGHT

Betty Beaty

Mills & Boon Classics

Betty Beaty

AMBER FIVE

Mills & Boon Classics

Essie Summers

SWEET ARE THE WAYS

Mills & Boon

Best Seller Romance

BEWARE
THE BEAST

Anne Mather

Mills & Boon

CHOOSE THE ONE YOU'LL MARRY

Mary Burchell

Mills & Boon

MASTER OF COMUS

Charlotte Lamb

Mills & Boon

BEST SELLER ROMANCE

High Tide
at Midnight

SARA CRAVEN

Mills & Boon

THE DEVIL AT ARCHANGEL

Sara Craven

Mills & Boon

TIDEWATER LOVER

Janet Dailey

1978

Janet Dailey
TIDEWATER LOVER
Mills & Boon

Mills & Boon

VALLEY OF THE MOON

Margaret Way

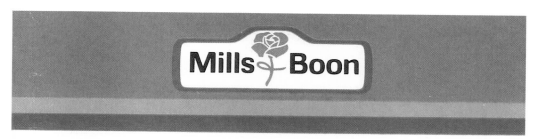

BEST SELLER ROMANCE

Dark
Master

CHARLOTTE LAMB

BEST SELLER ROMANCE

Possession

CHARLOTTE LAMB

1979

Charlotte Lamb
POSSESSION
Mills & Boon

182

Mills & Boon

APOLLO'S SEED

Anne Mather

1979

Anne Mather
APOLLO'S SEED
Mills & Boon

1979

Margery Hilton
TIME OF CURTAINFALL
Mills & Boon

Mills & Boon Classics

Margery Hilton

TIME OF CURTAINFALL

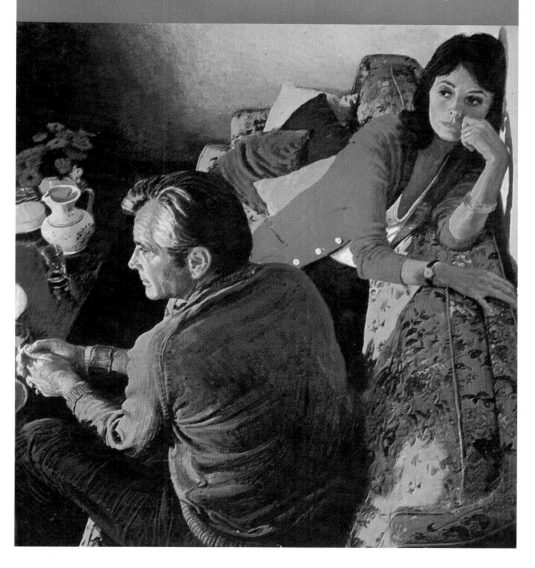

Mills & Boon

FRUSTRATION

Charlotte Lamb

1979
Charlotte Lamb
FRUSTRATION
Mills & Boon

Mills & Boon

WITH THIS RING

Mary Wibberley

Mills & Boon

COMPULSION

Charlotte Lamb

Mills & Boon

SAVAGE SURRENDER

Charlotte Lamb

EGYPTIAN HONEYMOON

MILLS & BOON

Elizabeth Ashton

1981

Elizabeth Ashton
EGYPTIAN HONEYMOON
Mills & Boon

Harlequin Romance

2410
1.25

Marriage in Haste

SUE PETERS

Harlequin Romance

2396
1.25

Where the Wolf Leads

JANE ARBOR

A SEASON FOR CHANGE

Margaret Way

FORGOTTEN LOVER

MILLS & BOON

Carole Mortimer

Mills & Boon

BEST SELLER ROMANCE

Daughter of Hassan

PENNY JORDAN

Mills & Boon

Romance

THE WOLF MAN

Sandra Clark

Mills & Boon Romance

RETURN TO YESTERDAY

Robyn Donald

Mills & Boon

Best Seller Romance

NOONFIRE

Margaret Way

1983

Margaret Way
NOONFIRE
Mills & Boon

Mills & Boon Romance

THE GIRL AT COBALT CREEK

Margaret Way

ROMANTIC PARTNERS COMPETITION
6 SOLITAIRE DIAMOND RINGS TO BE WON
SEE INSIDE BACK COVER FOR DETAILS

Mills & Boon

Romance

PAGAN ENCHANTMENT

Carole Mortimer

Mills & Boon

Romance

A FIERCE ENCOUNTER

Jane Donnelly

Mills & Boon

Romance

THE SLENDER THREAD

Yvonne Whittal

THE FAILED MARRIAGE

MILLS & BOON

Carole Mortimer

Mills & Boon

·ROMANCE·

Almost a Stranger

MARGARET WAY

1984

Margaret Way
ALMOST A STRANGER
Mills & Boon

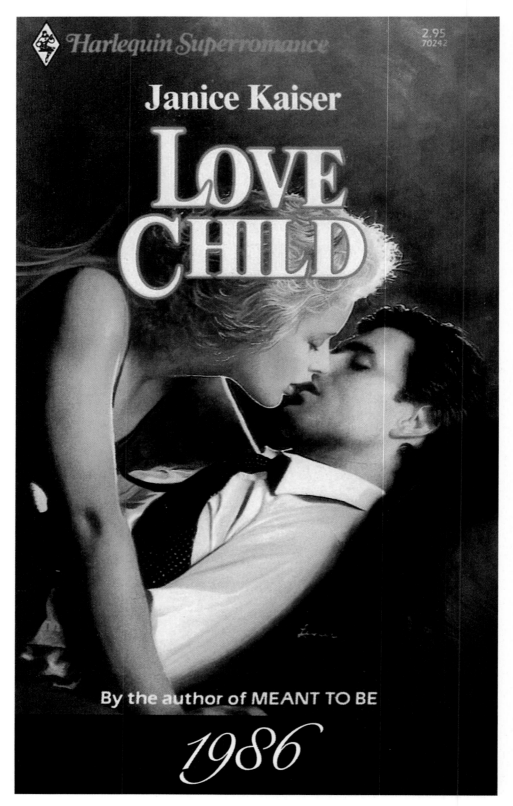

2.95
70242

Harlequin Superromance

Janice Kaiser

LOVE CHILD

By the author of MEANT TO BE

1986

Mills & Boon

ROMANCE

Diamond Valley

MARGARET WAY

INHERITANCE OF PASSION

1986

Margaret Way
DIAMOND VALLEY
Mills & Boon

205

ROMANCE

Capture a Shadow

LEIGH MICHAELS

Mills & Boon

ROMANCE

Hay Fever

MARY LYONS

COULD LOVE HEAL THEIR WOUNDS?

1987

Mary Lyons
HAY FEVER
Mills & Boon

Mills & Boon

BEST SELLER ROMANCE

An Old Passion

ROBYN DONALD

1988

Robyn Donald
AN OLD PASSION
Mills & Boon

208

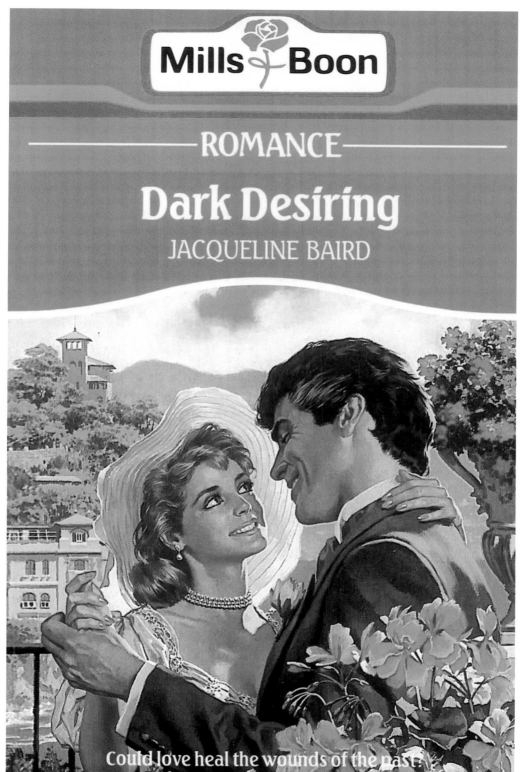

Mills & Boon

ROMANCE

Dark Desiring

JACQUELINE BAIRD

Could love heal the wounds of the past?

Mills & Boon

Sandra Marton

Fly Like an Eagle

1989

Sandra Marton
FLY LIKE AN EAGLE
Mills & Boon

210

Λόγος Ύπαρξης

ΠΕΝΥ ΤΖΟΡΝΤΑΝ

ΑΡΛΕΚΙΝ

Συλλογή

No 1003

1989

Penny Jordan
A REASON FOR BEING
Harlequin (Greek edition)

יסורי אהבה

פאני ג'ורדן

מהדורת יובל ה-40 של הוצאת

Harlequin

1989

Penny Jordan
A REASON FOR BEING
Harlequin (Hebrew edition)

Mills & Boon

Penny Jordan

A Reason for Being

SIMULTANEOUS WORLDWIDE PUBLICATION IN OVER **100** COUNTRIES

1989

Penny Jordan
A REASON FOR BEING
Mills & Boon

Mills & Boon

ROMANCE

A Christmas Affair

CAROLE MORTIMER

Mills & Boon

Emma Goldrick

The Girl He Left Behind

1990

Emma Goldrick
THE GIRL HE LEFT BEHIND
Mills & Boon

ROMANCE

Time to Let Go

ALISON FRASER

1990

Alison Fraser
TIME TO LET GO
Mills & Boon

216

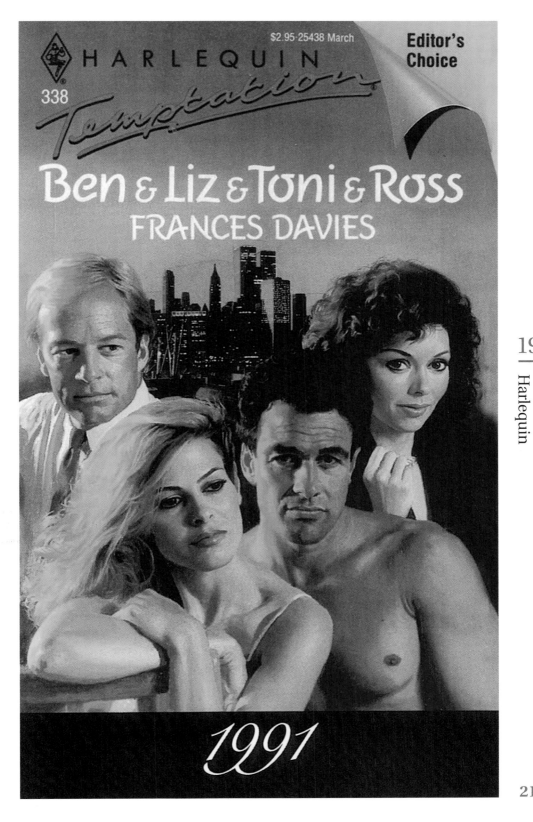

Mills & Boon

ROMANCE

No Gentle Seduction

HELEN BIANCHIN

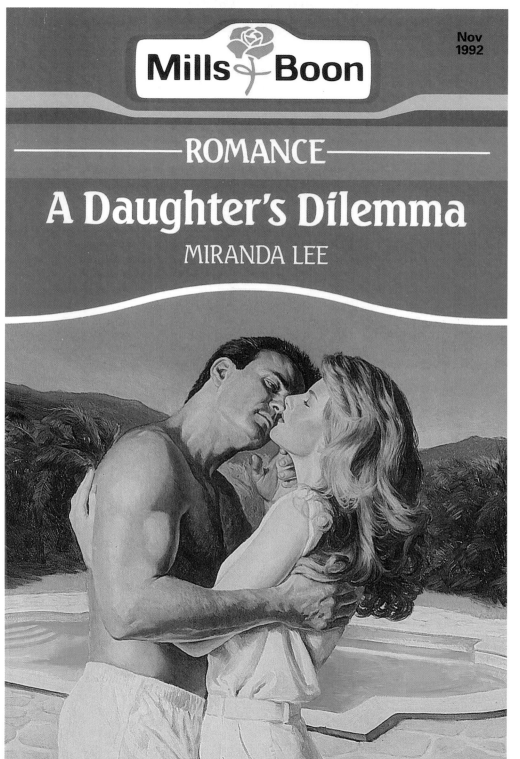

Nov
1992

Mills & Boon

ROMANCE

A Daughter's Dilemma

MIRANDA LEE

Mills & Boon

ROMANCE

A Family Affair

CHARLOTTE LAMB

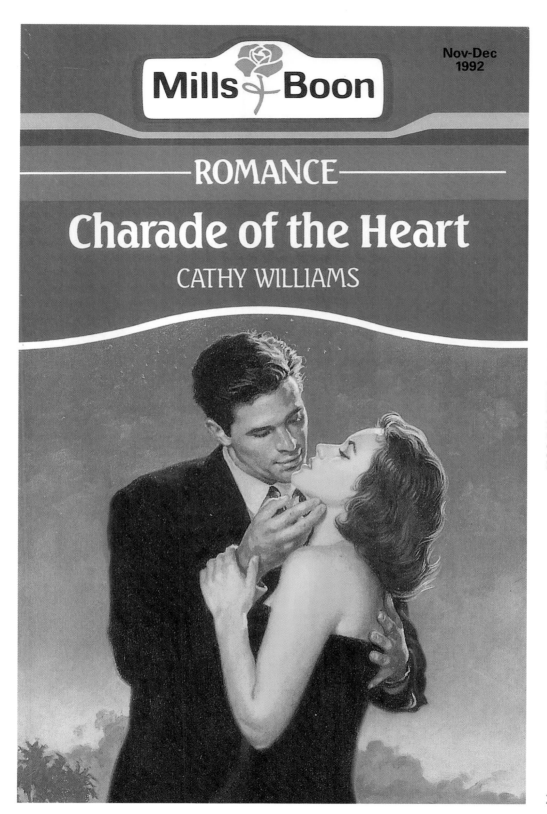

Nov-Dec
1992

Mills & Boon

ROMANCE

Charade of the Heart

CATHY WILLIAMS

Mills & Boon

Nov 1992

ROMANCE

Ride the Storm

EMMA DARCY

Dec
1992

Mills & Boon

ROMANCE

Secret Admirer

SUSAN NAPIER

MASQUERADE *Historical*

Nov
1992

THE CAPTAIN'S ANGEL

Marie-Louise Hall

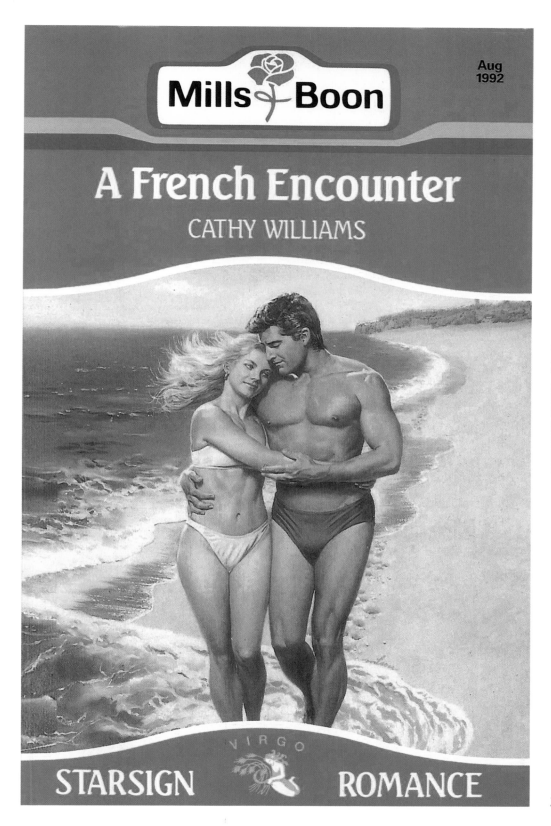

Aug
1992

Mills & Boon

A French Encounter
CATHY WILLIAMS

VIRGO

STARSIGN ROMANCE

Mills & Boon

ROMANCE

A Love Like That

NATALIE FOX

Mills & Boon

Sep 199?

ROMANCE

Fire in the Blood

CHARLOTTE LAMB

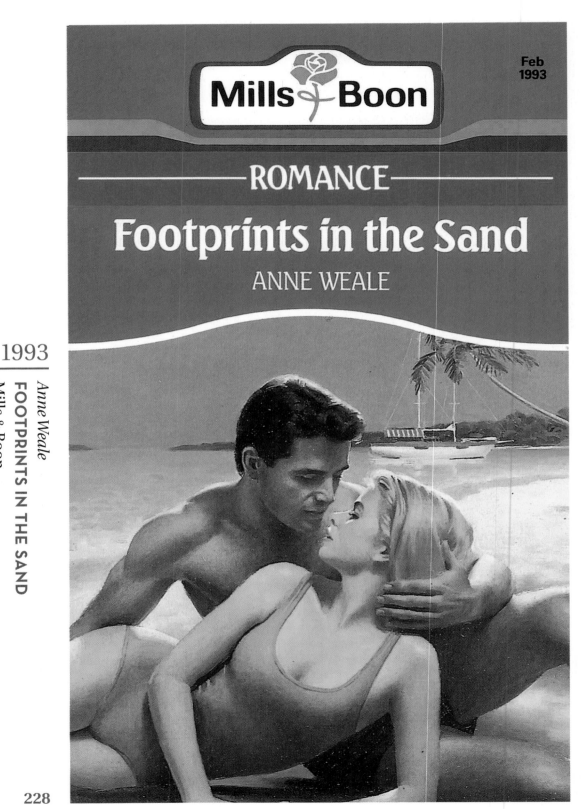

Feb
1993

Mills & Boon

ROMANCE

Footprints in the Sand

ANNE WEALE

Jul
1993

Mills & Boon

ROMANCE

Love's Fantasy

BARBARA McMAHON

Len Goldberg

1993

Barbara McMahon
LOVE'S FANTASY
Mills & Boon. Cover illustration by Len Goldberg

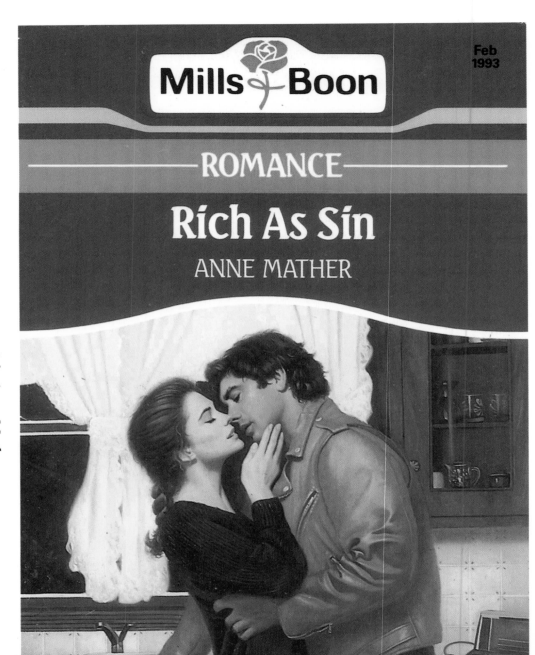

Feb 1993

Mills & Boon

ROMANCE

Rich As Sin

ANNE MATHER

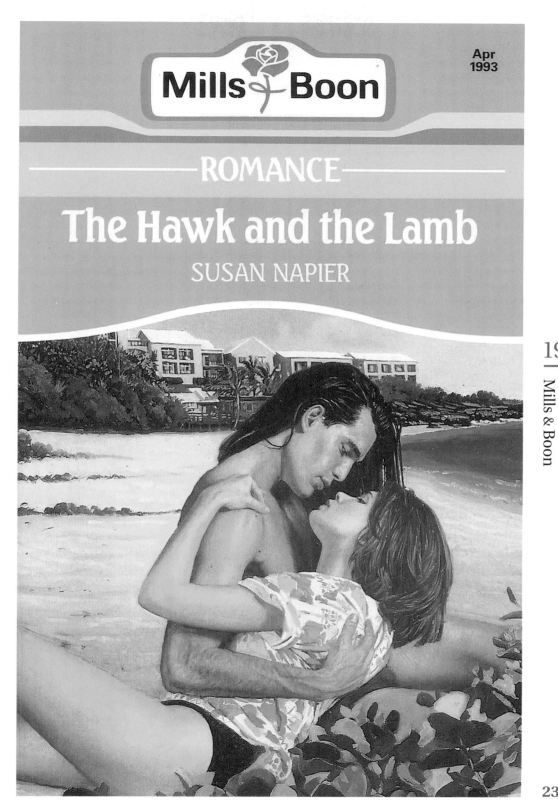

Mills & Boon

Apr 1993

ROMANCE

The Hawk and the Lamb

SUSAN NAPIER

May
1993

Mills & Boon

·ROMANCE·

The Spanish Connection

KAY THORPE

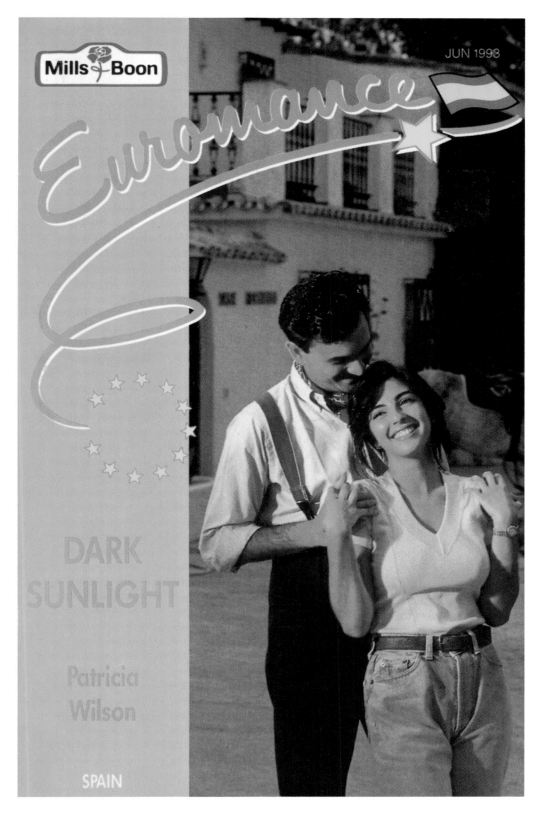

JUN 1998

Mills & Boon

Euromance

DARK
SUNLIGHT

Patricia
Wilson

SPAIN

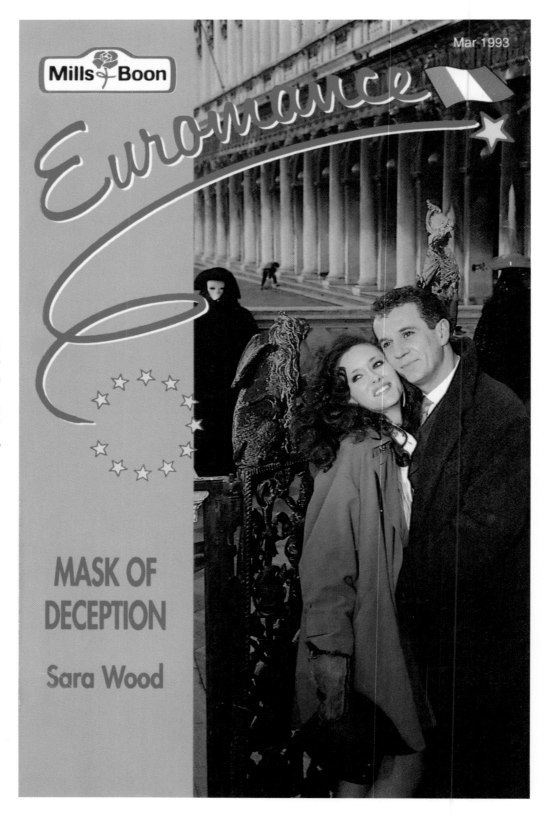

Mills & Boon

Euromance

Mar 1993

MASK OF DECEPTION

Sara Wood

R-1055

Harlequin Romances
ハーレクイン・ロマンス

憎いあなた

シャーロット・ラム

小林町子 訳

テムズ川
恋のゆくえⅠ

1994

Charlotte Lamb
BESIEGED
Harlequin KK (Japanese translation)

1995

Kate Walker
NO HOLDING BACK
Mills & Boon

No
Holding
Back

KATE WALKER

615

HARLEQUIN®
AMERICAN ROMANCE®

$3.50 U.S.
$3.99 CAN.
January

JACQUELINE DIAMOND

YOURS, MINE AND OURS

1996

1996

Jacqueline Diamond
YOURS, MINE AND OURS
Harlequin

MILLS & BOON®
Presents™

SHARON KENDRICK
One Bridegroom Required!

WANTED:
One Wedding
Dress

MILLS & BOON®

ROMANCE™

MISSION TO
SEDUCE

SALLY WENTWORTH

1998

Sally Wentworth
MISSION TO SEDUCE
Mills & Boon

R-1400

HARLEQUIN *Romances*

ハーレクイン・ロマンス

砂漠のドクター

ヴァイオレット・ウィンズピア／細郷妙子 訳

1998
Violet Winspear
DESERT DOCTOR
Harlequin KK (Japanese translation)

ハーレクイン・ロマンス1400号記念

240

THE HUSBAND CAMPAIGN

Barbara McMahon

1999

Barbara McMahon
THE HUSBAND CAMPAIGN
Mills & Boon

MILLS & BOON®

ROMANCE™

REFORM OF
THE PLAYBOY

MARY LYONS

MILLS & BOON

Penny Jordan

Taken by
the Sheikh

Modern
romance™

2006

Penny Jordan
TAKEN BY THE SHEIKH
Mills & Boon

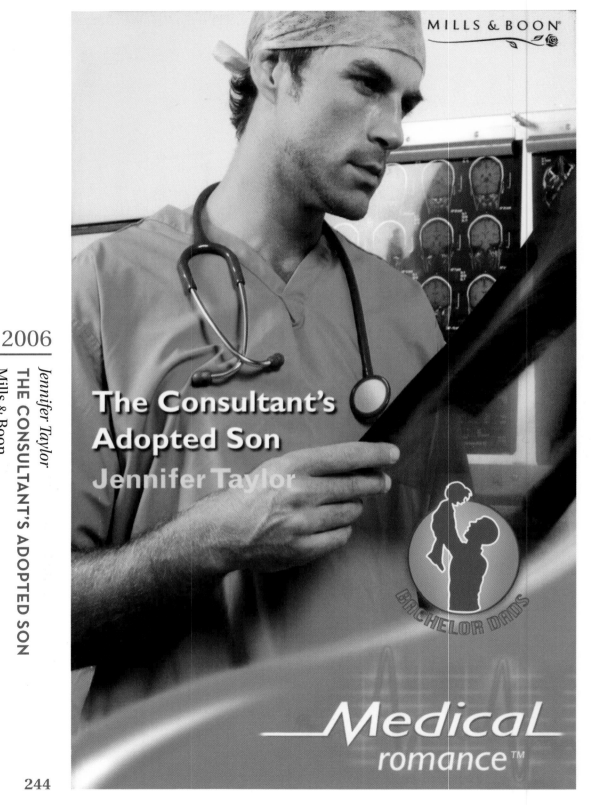

MILLS & BOON

The Consultant's
Adopted Son

Jennifer Taylor

BACHELOR DADS

Medical
romance™

Romantic **Suspense**

HQ COMICS

THE HEART OF A RULER

〈奪われた王冠Ⅰ〉

拒まれたプリンセス

マリー・フェラレーラ

岡田純子

2006

Marie Ferrarella
THE HEART OF A RULER
Harlequin KK (Japanese Manga Version)

THE MIGHTY QUINNS: MARCUS

Kate Hoffmann

2007

Kate Hoffmann
THE MIGHTY QUINNS: MARCUS
Mills & Boon

MILLS & BOON

100 YEARS
of pure reading pleasure

MILLS & BOON®

Blaze®

The Rebel King

Kathleen Creighton

NEW LOOK!

MILLS & BOON®
INTRIGUE

2007

Kathleen Creighton
THE REBEL KING
Mills & Boon

Pure Romance

 HQ comics

THIS MAN AND THIS WOMAN

花嫁には秘密

ルーシー・ゴードン

碧 ゆかこ

2007

Lucy Gordon
THIS MAN AND THIS WOMAN
Harlequin KK (Japanese Manga Version)

KIMANI ROMANCE

Never Without

You...

Again

FRANCINE CRAFT

2007

Francine Craft
**NEVER WITHOUT
YOU...AGAIN**
Harlequin. Cover design by Camden Leeds

249

MILLS & BOON

9½ Days
Mia Zachary

Blaze™

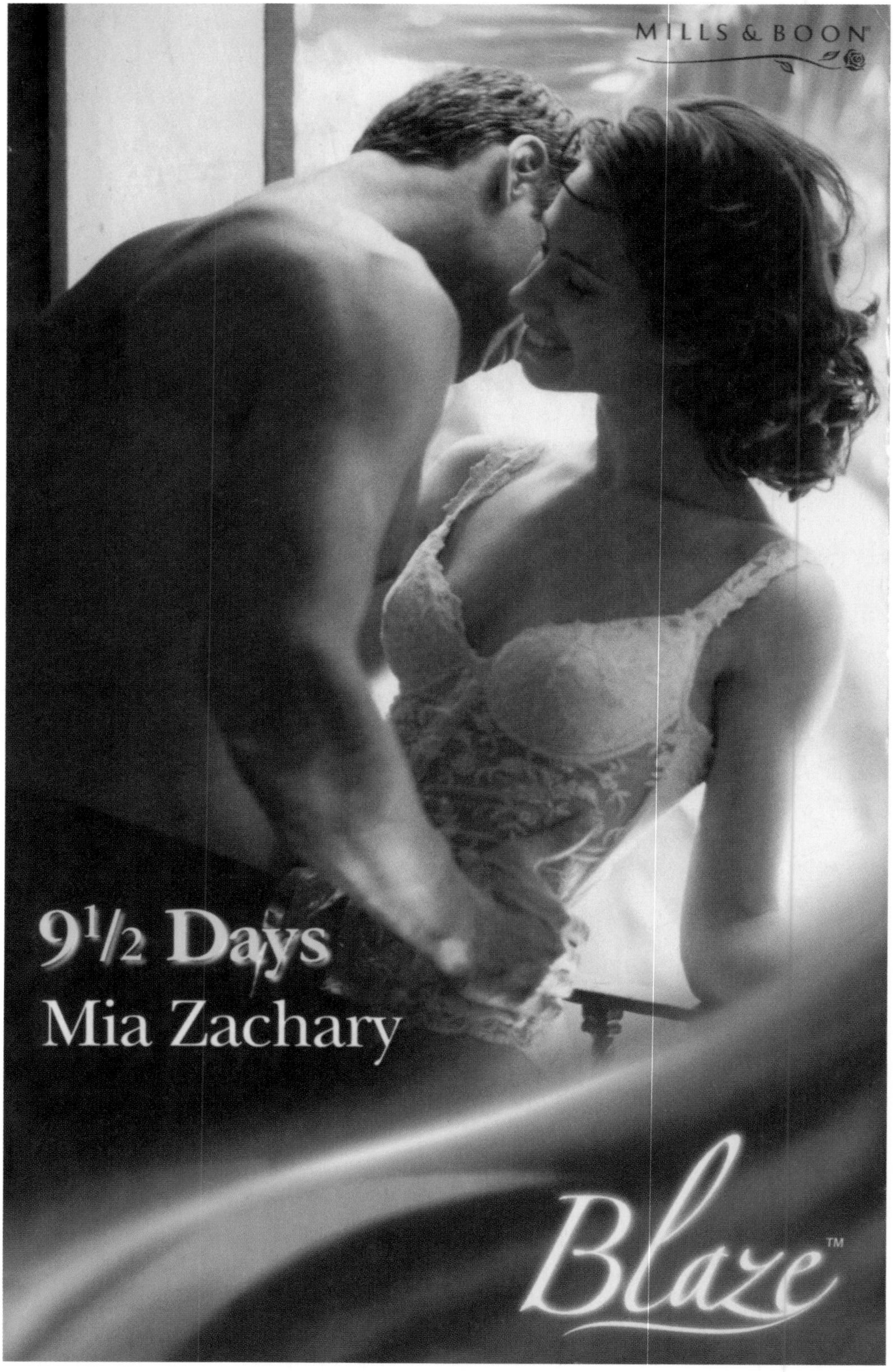

HARLEQUIN *Romans*®

NR 12 06/08 INDEKS 360325 CENA 7,99 ZŁ W TYM 0% VAT

Jak w bajce
miniseria

Susan Meier
Długo i szczęśliwie

2008

Susan Meier
DŁUGO I SZCZĘŚLIWIE (TWICE A PRINCESS)
Arlekin Wydawnictwo (Harlequin Romans)

251

His Majesty's Mistress

Robyn Donald

MILLS & BOON
100 YEARS
of pure reading pleasure

MILLS & BOON®
MODERN™

The Guardian's Forbidden Mistress

Miranda Lee

100TH BIRTHDAY EDITION

FREE BONUS STORY

MILLS & BOON
MODERN